THE DEPORTATION CASES
OF 1919-1920

A Da Capo Press Reprint Series

CIVIL LIBERTIES IN AMERICAN HISTORY

GENERAL EDITOR: LEONARD W. LEVY

Brandeis University

THE DEPORTATION CASES
OF 1919-1920

BY CONSTANTINE M. PANUNZIO

DA CAPO PRESS · NEW YORK · 1970

A Da Capo Press Reprint Edition

This Da Capo Press edition of *The Deportation Cases of 1919-1920* is an unabridged republication of the first edition published in New York in 1921.

Library of Congress Catalog Card Number 77-109547

SBN 306-71901-0

Published by Da Capo Press
A Division of Plenum Publishing Corporation
227 West 17th Street, New York, N.Y. 10011

Manufactured in the United States of America

The
Deportation Cases
of 1919-1920

A Study by

CONSTANTINE M. PANUNZIO, M. A.

COMMISSION ON THE CHURCH
AND SOCIAL SERVICE

FEDERAL COUNCIL OF THE CHURCHES
OF CHRIST IN AMERICA
105 EAST 22nd STREET, NEW YORK

CONTENTS

CHAPTER   PAGE

      INTRODUCTION 5

      AUTHOR'S PREFACE 9

  I WHAT THE DEPORTATION LAWS PROVIDE... 13

  II WHO THE ARRESTED ALIENS WERE....... 17

  III HOW THE ARRESTS WERE MADE.......... 24

  IV HOW THE ALIENS WERE TRIED........... 35

  V HOW MANY WERE CONNECTED WITH PRO-
      SCRIBED ORGANIZATIONS 50

  VI HOW THE ALIENS FELT ABOUT LEAVING
      AMERICA 72

  VII HOW THE ALIENS WERE TREATED......... 77

  VIII HOW LONG THE ALIENS WERE HELD IN
      PRISON 83

  IX HOW THE ALIENS' FAMILIES WERE AF-
      FECTED 89

  X SUMMARY 93

      APPENDIX

      I Excerpts from the Deportation Laws
         Affecting Alien Anarchists...... 99

      II Statistics 101

INTRODUCTION

Since the beginning of our participation in the World War, the American people have become aware of an unwholesome situation occasioned by the absence of close understanding and sympathy between the main body of our people and large numbers of its immigrant population. Enough has been said of the inadequacy both in conception and in execution of our many "Americanization" plans but the study which here follows inevitably draws attention to a fundamental difficulty in the status both in law and in custom which the alien occupies as a resident in this country.

The study here presented embodies the findings of an investigation into the recent deportations of persons deemed to be unlawfully in the country, under the anarchist provisions of the Immigration Law.[1] Its purpose is to call public attention to practices that are inconsistent with the American tradition of justice and fair-play. The data here recorded concerning the deportation of aliens reveal the necessity for thoroughgoing reforms. The author is a minister of the Methodist Episcopal Church, who is a student of immigrant problems and has served churches in immigrant communities. Though not directly responsible for the study, the Commission on the Church and Social Service has been in close touch with it from the beginning. The data have been carefully examined and the report has been edited by the Research Department.

It should also be stated that in this introductory word

---

[1] See Appendix I.

no attempt is made to arrive at what might be called an entirely adequate method of dealing with alien political offenders. It may be that the developing conscience of the nation will demand changes which it is at present quite impossible to secure. Many persons feel that deportation is essentially an evasion of moral responsibility. Christians look upon international relationships as opportunities for mutual service. It may well be argued that the very concept of Christendom renders deportations from one nation to another wholly anomalous. But we are here concerned only with practical proposals for a legislative program, and the aim is to indicate concrete reforms upon which we are warranted in believing that general agreement can presently be arrived at.

The following proposals are offered, not dogmatically, but as a tentative basis for a seriously needed modification of the present law. They have been formulated after extensive consideration of the problems involved by persons of wide experience and authoritative opinions.

1. With reference to what are commonly called political offenses, no act or utterance which at common law would not amount to a solicitation or attempt to commit a crime should be held a sufficient ground for deportation. To deport a person merely for the possession of ideas, however objectionable, is not only an illiberal, but a wholly futile, method of directing intellectual development.

2. It seems clear that the interests of equal justice would be promoted by eliminating from the Immigration Law the provision which makes membership in certain organizations a sufficient cause for deportation. The report makes it evident that the status of an individual alien in relation to the Government cannot with safety be determined on the basis of membership in an organ-

ization. Without reference to the controversy over the legality of this or that organization, "membership" is too ill-defined a relationship to be made the exclusive test of an individual's attitude.

3. An alien resident after he has been in the country for a period long enough to allow of a full determination of his right to domicile in the United States should, when his deportation is sought for any cause, have the protection of such due process of law and of such constitutional safeguards as apply to a citizen accused of a crime.

4. There seems to be no unanimity of opinion among authorities on immigration as to whether or not deportation cases should be handled entirely by the Federal Courts. A possible alternative would be an immigration court, quasi-judicial in character, in which the alien would be guaranteed due process of law and the proper constitutional safeguards.

5. It cannot be doubted that the method of raiding recently employed in apprehending suspected aliens has resulted in great injustice and hardship. These evils would be effectually prevented by a provision that arrests should be made only when a warrant has previously been sworn out and is served by the officer making the arrest, or when the offense is committed in the presence of the officer.

6. The Government agent, who himself instigates unlawful acts for the purpose of apprehending the perpetrators, protecting himself by his official connection, must be eliminated from the administration of our federal laws. Two measures suggest themselves as tending to curb such activities.

a. A provision that no agent who is found to have

provoked unlawful acts shall be granted immunity on the ground of his Government connection.

b. A provision that no person shall be convicted on evidence that shows him to have been incited by a provocative agent to the offense of which he is accused.

The Commission believes that the evils at which these suggested reforms are directed are of first magnitude and should at once engage the attention of the public and of Congress.

COMMISSION ON THE CHURCH AND SOCIAL SERVICE

AUTHOR'S PREFACE

In the autumn and winter of 1919-1920 an extraordinary number of foreign-born persons residing in the United States left this country for Europe. During the out-going movement the American people were frequently discussing the reasons why these "foreigners" were leaving this country. While the exodus was at its height I made a trip to Europe in order to learn at first-hand from the emigrants themselves the reasons for this unprecedented outflow. In order to do this all the more directly I transformed myself into an emigrant and travelled steerage and thereby had an opportunity freely to question the emigrants. In the course of the voyage and on the continent eighty persons were questioned, some of whom were interviewed several times, and careful notes were made after each interview. Naturally I had expected to find the usual reasons given, namely, that they were going to Europe to visit their people, or that they had some business to look after or were going to get their families and return to this country. On tabulating the findings, however, I found that a large proportion had mentioned what they termed "persecution," or "repression." Of the Americans in general they said, "They don't want foreigners." This revelation became all the more forceful when upon reaching the continent I found a little book in circulation entitled, "The End of America," in which the author with some measure of accuracy describes conditions in this country and maintains that the America of men's dreams is fast vanishing from the earth.* All of this was naturally offensive to me, for, though of foreign birth myself, I have been an American citizen for several years and have come to feel admiration and love for America and for American life.

---

* For full report see article by author in *World Outlook*, May, 1920, or *Literary Digest*, June 19, 1920.

9

While still in Europe, therefore, I decided to make a careful study of the facts involved in the contention made by the emigrants, that foreign born residents in America were suffering persecution. A peculiar coincidence afforded an opportunity to make this study. On the return voyage, in the middle of December, 1919, the ship's bulletin carried the news of the raids which had been made on the Union of Russian Workers and of the arrest of thousands of foreigners. On landing I found the press carrying large headlines on the subject and giving full pages to it. Soon after that, on December 21, 249 aliens, alleged to be radicals, were deported on the S. S. "Buford." In the early part of 1920 other raids took place and the country heard for months of the impending danger arising from the immigrants in this country.

All this furnished an occasion for a thorogoing study. Accordingly, in early February, 1920, I began the study, the results of which are recorded in these pages. First: Immigrant communities were visited and certain leaders were interviewed. Second: By permission of the United States Department of Labor, four prisons or detention stations were visited:—the Hartford (Conn.) County Jail, the Youngstown (Ohio), and the Pittsburgh (Pa.) prisons and the detention camp at Detroit. In these prison investigations 168 alien prisoners were interviewed. Third: 200 official records of the hearings in deportation proceedings were examined. These papers, which are on file with the Department of Labor, are the regular and only official records.

What follows concerning the aliens who were arrested as deportable persons is based on a very careful and thorough examination of two hundred records in the offices of the Department of Labor, covering the full proceedings in the cases involved. If this study has any particular merit it grows out of the manner in which this examination was made. In order to avoid the possibility of a non-representative selection, permission was secured to examine any or all of the records which passed through the office from day to day. This method insured a balanced and trustworthy study. It yielded in the first place a fair proportion of each of the classes enumerated; it furnished a large variety of cases as well as a complete geographical distribution.[1] It also afforded an opportunity to study the aliens in various cities under various inspectors. What is presented, therefore, is a representative cross-section, so to speak, of the great mass of deportation cases.

To supplement the official records, the results of prison interviews are here and there introduced, not only by way of corroboration, but for the human elements with which they enliven the documents. Unless otherwise indicated, however, the quotations cited are taken from the records themselves and may be verified at will.

These records are kept on file with the Bureau of Immigration. They form the most valuable sources of information regarding the personal character and history of the aliens. If the proceedings have been properly conducted these official records include the following items:

1. The original affidavit of probable cause by an agent of the Department of Justice.
2. A carbon copy of the original warrant of arrest.
3. The record of the preliminary examination given the alien at the time of arrest.
4. A complete official transcript of all the proceedings in the case and of testimonies given in regular hearing, or hearings, conducted by the Immigration Inspector.
5. A summary of findings and recommendations by the local Immigration Inspector.
6. A summary of findings and recommendations by the Commissioner-General of Immigration.
7. Actual evidence or record of evidence submitted in the case.
8. A record of bail when secured.
9. A brief submitted by the alien's attorney.
10. Letters submitted by the alien's friends and employers.

---
[1] See Appendix II, D.

11. A memorandum from the Secretary of Labor or his representative giving final decision on the case together with
instructions for disposition.

The records are not always complete, as will presently
appear, but in the majority of cases they include all of
the items above enumerated.

In order to make a complete abstract of all the information contained in these records a blank was prepared
covering the various captions indicated in the chapter
headings of this study.

The investigation yielded a vast amount of important
material which, though it was not feasible to embody it
in this study, it is my hope to bring out in some other
form. However, the following pages contain all the matter essential to the purposes of this volume.

The reader of this document should bear in mind that
it has no relation whatever to political controversy. The
results recorded are simply a statement of fact. The
facts have been secured at first-hand. The human as-
pects of the situation have had first consideration and
the legal phases of the subject have been considered
secondarily.

I wish to express gratitude to the Federal authorities
at the various prisons and in Washington for the willing-
ness and the uniform courtesy with which they furnished
the needed information; more particularly to the authorities of the Department of Labor for giving free access
to the official records of hearings, without which this
study could not have been possible. Acknowledgment
is also made to the Rev. Clyde F. Armitage and Miss
Agnes H. Campbell for invaluable assistance given by
them in the collection of the data; to Miss Grace W. Sims
and Miss Mabel A. Brown for their untiring effort in
connection with the investigation and the tabulation of
the results.

C. M. PANUNZIO.

White Plains, N. Y.,
January 1st, 1921

CHAPTER I

WHAT THE DEPORTATION LAWS PROVIDE

The Law

The arrests and deportations which furnish the matter of this study were instituted under statutes which constitute part of a great body of Immigration Law of the United States. In order that our national policy in the matter of exclusion and deportation of politically undesirable aliens may be fully understood, it is necessary to examine briefly the provisions of the several enactments on which it rests.

The first Act of Congress to make provision for the exclusion of persons whose political views were obnoxious was that of March 3, 1903, where "anarchists" are included in the list of persons excluded from entry into the United States. The Act of Feberuary 20, 1907, re-enacted this clause, and the immigration Act of February 5, 1917, extended the scope of the previous laws by making provision for the *expulsion* of anarchists as well as for their exclusion, and removed the statutory limitation of a five-year period within which deportation can be effected.* This Act of February 5, 1917, was amended further by the Act of October 16, 1918, which provides for expulsion and exclusion not only of anarchists but of aliens teaching or advocating the overthrow by force or violence of the Government of the United States.

The Proceedings

By the terms of the statute the Secretary of Labor is made solely responsible for its administration. The usual requirements of criminal court procedure do not apply

---

* See Excerpts from Immigration Law: Appendix I.   This law was further strengthened by the act of June 5, 1920.

in deportation cases, which the Supreme Court has held to be administrative rather than judicial. Such part as may properly be taken by the Department of Justice is confined to gathering evidence and submitting findings. The statutes recognize no authority residing in any officials of the government save those of the Department of Labor.

The proceedings by which resident aliens alleged to be in the country in violation of the law are taken into custody, are known as "legal warrant proceedings." These proceedings have three distinct steps:

FIRST: Evidence of probable cause is submitted to the Secretary of Labor or his representative in a sworn statement by an officer of the Government who knows the facts or has reason to believe the charge; or by affidavit of such officer made upon personal knowledge or information and belief. The Secretary of Labor or his representative examines the statement or the affidavit, and, if he is convinced that the alien is in the country unlawfully, he then issues a warrant of arrest and the alien is apprehended and placed in the custody of a local immigration officer.

SECOND: This warrant, when regular procedure is followed, is served by authorized agents of the Department of Labor, who upon apprehending the alien give him what is known as a preliminary examination, and place him in the custody of the Immigration Inspector. While in the custody of the latter, the alien is given an administrative hearing. He is entitled to counsel in his effort to prove the charges false. The burden of proof rests upon him. A verbatim report is taken of the hearing by an official stenographer which is forwarded to the Secretary of Labor.

THIRD: The Secretary examines the records of the

hearing, etc., and the corroborative evidence submitted and renders a decision, either for cancellation of the warrant or for issuance of a deportation warrant. If the decision is in favor of the alien on the ground that the evidence does not sustain the charges, he endorses the papers "Cancel." The word "Cancel" in this connection is equivalent to a verdict in a criminal case, of "Not guilty." If the decision is against the alien, the present custom of the Secretary of Labor or his representative is to endorse the papers "Deport." The alien then is taken to an immigrant detention station and deported as soon as possible.

The Inspector

Since the chief factor in the actual, local administration of the law in deportation cases is the immigration inspector, it is important that a word be said about this official and the part which he plays. The immigrant inspectorship is open to every male citizen of the United States who has passed his twentieth but has not reached his fifty-first birthday. The requirements of the Civil Service Commission for the immigrant inspectorship include an examination in spelling, arithmetic, penmanship, letter writing, copying from plain copy, practical questions on immigration law and general education, training and experience. The applicant is not required to have any knowledge of law, of languages other than English, nor to have had any practical experience in the handling of groups of immigrants. One of the latest circulars of the United States Civil Service Commission, however, states, "It is desired to secure persons who have had practical experience in handling and dealing with the public and who have had positions of responsibility where they were required to exercise good judgment in emergencies." A large proportion of these inspectors are receiving the minimum salary of $1,380 a year plus the bonus of $240.

The Cases of 1919-1920

Since, by the terms of the law, membership on the part of an alien in an organization which entertains a belief in the overthrow of the Government of the United States, or all government, by force or violence, is in itself ground for deportation, the Secretary of Labor felt called upon to make a ruling concerning the Communist Party. On January 24, 1920, he issued such a ruling, declaring that any alien member of the Communist Party was *ipso facto* illegally in the country.* The administration of the law in such cases was therefore simply a matter of establishing the suspect's membership in the proscribed organization. It was concerning the interpretation of "membership" that a sharp controversy has arisen over the decisions reached by the Secretary of Labor in a large number of these cases. This report is not concerned with the controversy, but aims at bringing out the essential facts of the entire proceeding.

Between November 1, 1919, and April 26, 1920, warrants were issued by the Department of Labor for the arrest of 6,350 aliens who were alleged to be in the country in violation of the law. Approximately 3,000 of these arrests were made. Of these, about 2,500 were alleged members of the Communist Party, and the remainder were alleged members of the Union of Russian Workers. After the customary hearings 762 persons were ordered deported—455 Communists and 307 members of the Union of Russian Workers. The actual deportations between the dates named numbered 271, of whom 249 were carried by the "Buford" on December 21, 1919, and 22 were deported subsequently.

---

* It was taken for granted that the Union of Russian Workers belonged in the same class.

CHAPTER II

WHO THE ARRESTED ALIENS WERE

Personnel of the Alien Groups

Naturally, in discussing these aliens the first questions of interest and of importance concern their personal history. Who were they? To what racial groups did they belong? What was their economic status? Were they educated or illiterate? Had they sought citizenship? What attitude did they take during the war?

Nationality

Of the 200 cases whose records were examined, 7 were women and 1 was a minor. Ten nationalities were represented in the list. One hundred forty-eight or 74 per cent were Russians.[1] Next in number came the Poles[2] with 19 or 9.5 per cent, the Lithuanians with 9 or 4.5 per cent, the Austrians with 8 or 4 per cent, the Croatians with 6 or 3 per cent. There were also 3 Germans, 2 Jugo-Slavs, 2 Hungarians, 1 Italian, 1 Bulgarian and 1 Hollander.[3]

In the case of one the nationality was not recorded.[3]

In considering the number of Russians, attention may be called to the fact that a large number of Russians in this country have been seeking for nearly five years an opportunity to communicate with their families or to return to Russia. They have not been able to procure passports on account of the political situation. This has made for uneasiness among them.

Age

The ages of the aliens ranged from 18 to 65 years. The greatest number were between 26 and 30 years. One

---

[1] Russians and Ukranians grouped together.
[2] Poles and Galicians grouped together.
[3] See Appendix II, A.

hundred seventy-nine or 89.5 per cent of the total number, were between 20 and 40 years of age. There was one boy of 19 years who was arrested at night school and found to be a member of the Union of Russian Workers.[1]

Residence in the United States

One hundred thirty-four or 67 per cent of the 200 aliens had been resident in this country from 6 to 10 years. Thirty-one or 15.5 per cent had been in this country from 1 to 5 years, while 23 or 11.5 per cent had been in America from 11 to 15 years. Seven had resided in this country from 16 to 20 years, and 1 had been here for 36 years. In 4 cases length of residence was not given.[2]

Marital Status

One hundred twelve, or 56 per cent, of these 200 persons were married. Seventy-four of these had children. Two men had 5 children, all born in the United States. One man had 6 children, 4 of whom were born in America; 2 spoke of having American-born wives, although they were not usually questioned on that subject. Twenty-one married men had families in the Old World, while 89 had families in the United States.

The total number of children involved in the 200 cases was 156, of whom 98 were born in this country and were living here.[3]

Knowledge of English

The knowledge of English which these persons possessed varied of course with the degree of their general intelligence. There were among them some very bright

---

[1] See Appendix II, B.
[2] See Appendix II, Table I.
[3] See Appendix II, C.

and intelligent young men who though they had been in the United States for only five or six years, still had mastered the language unusually well. Others, though they had been here longer, could speak scarcely any English. In the prison investigations it was found that a large majority could understand and make themselves understood through the medium of the English language. The official records show that in 78 cases an interpreter was employed in the course of the hearing, in 23 cases no interpreter was used, while in 99 cases no record is found in regard to the presence of an interpreter. It goes almost without saying that these persons were insured of a fair degree of just treatment in proportion as they could or could not make themselves understood.

There were a few who aside from inability to speak English were illiterate with respect to their own language.

Status Relative to Citizenship

As has been already stated, of the 200 cases examined, 7 were women. One was a minor. There were therefore 192 concerning whom the question of citizenship might be raised. Of this number there were 26 cases in which no record as to citizenship was found. Of the remaining 166 persons, 54 had made application for first papers.* Frequent statements record difficulties encountered by these aliens in obtaining citizenship. One man, Rudolph Sarpu (Warrant No. 54860/750), stated:

"In New London it is impossible to get papers, because there is no place where they give them, but I went with another fellow to Norwich. We took the day off and went to take out first papers. They said, 'Here's a form; you fill it out and bring it back.' That was on March 27, 1919. Since I had to lose time, it was impossible for me to do it, so I never brought them back."

Nine men said they had been told that they could not get first papers unless they could read and write, and

---

* See Appendix II, Table I.

one man said he was told that if he took out papers they would never let him out of this country. (Warrant No. 54709/399.) Six aliens promised during the proceedings to become citizens if allowed to remain in this country. The statement of R. Sieman (Warrant No. 54810/1) is typical of this feeling. He said:

> "I am through with everything. I will learn to read and write, get my papers and be a citizen, work hard and get an education for my children and family; that is all."

War Records

The war record of the alien was frequently omitted. However, 37 are recorded as having purchased Liberty bonds and 24 as having bought thrift stamps or contributed to some patriotic fund. Two of the alleged radicals who were arrested and held for deportation had actually served in the United States Army. In the case of Steve Kerekoff (Warrant No. 54860/156), a certified copy of his honorable discharge from the Army was introduced in the alien's defense. When questioned as to the organization of which he was a member, he replied, "The American Legion." His personal effects consisted of a suitcase and an Army uniform.

Record is also found that three of these alleged radicals had waived their right to exemption when registering for the draft and one had volunteered but had been refused because of physical disability. In one case an "Aircraft Industrial Service" Army button was introduced into the evidence as proof of the loyalty of the alien. Many of the men, whose cases were examined, were beyond the age of military service. Ernest Behm (Warrant No. 54735/102), a man 50 years of age, said that his eldest son had volunteered and had served in the United States Naval Reserve.

One man who was deported had been very active in

Liberty Loan Drives and an ardent advocate of Americanism among his Russian fellow countrymen.

In connection with the prison investigations four ex-soldiers were found at Detroit among those being held on a charge of belief in the overthrow by force of the United States Government. These men were Poles, and each had received his honorable discharge from the Army. One had served seventeen months in France and had been discharged because of disability. He had made application for citizenship while in France and remarked to the investigator: "They did not kill me in France; they get me here." A second had served twelve months at the front, and the other two had been in service five months each. Two of them had experienced difficulty in finding work after leaving the army; one had been out of work for five months. Still another man said when interviewed, that he had tried to join the army, but had been rejected. He had volunteered for Government service and had his badge and certificate to prove this.

Occupation and Economic Status

Occupationally these persons represented the average run of immigrants in America. They were steel and brass workers, carpenters, painters, printers, restaurant waiters, teamsters, mechanics, shoemakers and manual laborers. In over half of the cases no reference is found to the economic status of those studied. In only nineteen of the records is it stated that the individual had no money. On the other hand forty-five persons were found to have sums ranging from a few dollars to $2,000. The money was usually in a savings bank, but one man kept his savings in a Prince Albert tobacco box and one stated that his wife was his savings bank.

A number had interests in various kinds of business.

One man had an interest in an ice and coal business; one owned stock in a mining concern and another in a motor truck company. One man owned an automobile, two persons owned a home, nearly paid for, while two others owned grocery businesses worth $2,000 and $7,000 respectively. Another man referred to his having lost $1,700 in a business enterprise. The prison investigations showed similarly a considerable range in economic status.

Four men stated that they had lost all they had since being arrested; one of these had given power of attorney to a fellow-countryman who had taken all the money and disappeared.

A Personal Testimony

It may be added that in some cases, both in the prison investigations and in the examination of the records, employers, social service agents, pastors, and even a deputy sheriff, immigration inspectors and department of justice agents spoke well of the men. In the case of four persons, a representative of the Ford plant in Detroit, where they had been employed, stated that he had always considered the men good workmen. An official physician at a certain detention station in a letter to the author, dated May 11, 1920, sums up the opinion of many persons who came into personal contact with the alleged radicals. This physician had had personal charge of all the aliens while they were being held pending their hearing or their deportation. I quote from his letter:

"Most of them impressed me as rather ordinary foreign workmen, a grade above altogether unskilled labor, of fair intelligence. A few had more intelligence and some were quite pleasant. A few also were obstinate, unreasonable, grouchy and generally unpleasant. The few with whom I talked had fairly radical ideas of social change, advanced with varying degrees of skill. I never was able to corner anyone into an admission of a program of violence. None of the men pressed his views upon me until approached, and then only as a matter of statement. They quite resented some clerk's error in referring to them as anarchists. Order was kept fairly easily. The radicals chose their own committees, through whom they dealt with the authorities. They made rules for their own conduct.

"They complained occasionally of their food and the sanitation of their quarters; most of these complaints had at least some ground. I never heard of any violence against their guards or attempt at it.

"In general, a few of these people I should not care to have around me at all; they are a general nuisance. Most of them seem harmless."

Cases of Women Arrested

Because of the social consequences involved, a general statement should be made at this point concerning the women who were included in these groups of aliens. Of the 200 cases examined, 7 were women. The husbands of 5 of them were also under arrest. The nationality record shows 4 to be Russian, 2 Polish and 1 Dutch. They had been in the United States for periods of from five to fifteen years, but their knowledge of English was slight. One woman could speak Russian, Lithuanian and German but handled English very imperfectly. All but one were mothers, and one was pregnant at the time of the hearing. Of the 12 children involved 10 were born in the United States.

Confronted with the possibility of deportation, the women whose husbands were also being held wanted to be with their husbands, no matter what their fate might be. All asked to be allowed to take their children with them, with the exception of one woman who was willing to sacrifice her children if they might have the advantage of living in America with their father.

CHAPTER III

HOW THE ARRESTS WERE MADE

The Raids

The exact number of arrests made in connection with deportation proceedings during the five-month period covered by this study is not known. It is certain, however, that the total number of aliens arrested between November, 1919, and March, 1920, greatly exceeded the number of warrants issued.

Arrests were made in two ways—by raids and by individual apprehension. Of the 200 cases here studied 169 were arrested in raids. There were two principal raids. One was conducted on November 7, 1919, against the Union of Russian Workers. The second took place on January 2, 1920, against the Communist Party of America.

These raids, or round-ups, as they are commonly called, were conducted by special agents. In some cases they were conducted with the aid of local police and in still other cases with the aid of specially sworn deputies and citizens and were aimed at meeting places of radical organizations, halls, schools, and other places where aliens were accustomed to congregate.* Usually all the men found in any of these places were arrested at the same time. As will be seen later, in many cases there were no warrants of arrest.

The homes of some suspected persons were also entered and searched. In one case a printing shop was entered and searched. In the case of Mike Stechna (Warrant 54810/490), it was shown during the hearing that search warrants were issued by authority of Chief Magistrate William McAdoo of New York City, giving

* Cf. Warrant Nos. 54859/530; 54860/669; 54860/283.

authority to certain police officers and state troopers to enter homes and meeting places.

The raid on the People's House in New York City on November 7, 1919, is particularly noteworthy. On one of the floors of this house a school was conducted by the Union of Russian Workers where various elementary subjects, languages, electrical and other trade subjects were said to have been taught. On the night in question the school was entered and a number of aliens attending the classes there were arrested. The manner in which this raid was conducted is told in a sworn statement by Tony Korscheikoff (Warrant No. 54709/455) who testified that he was studying arithmetic when the detectives and policemen came in and ordered them all down stairs. On the way down they had to pass a line of men, each of whom hit the passerby with a club or a blackjack. Harry Skochuk (Warrant No. 54709/447) testified also that about thirty students were locked in a room, searched, driven downstairs, beaten and hit by policemen as they passed, and carried in patrol wagons to the police station. This man further testified that laundry checks, school cards and insurance papers were taken from him. Other cases showing similar treatment of arrested aliens will be found in Chapter VII.

Warrants for Arrest

The law requires that warrants for the arrest of aliens who are presumed to be illegally in the country shall issue from the Department of Labor. It is common practice, as every one knows, to arrest for felonies without warrant, and raids are also frequently made on gambling houses, for example, without warrant either for search or for arrest. This rather loose practice is debatable even in the enforcement of the criminal law, save where the offender is taken in the act of committing a crime, in which case even a civilian may make an arrest. But as applied in non-criminal proceedings there is room for the contention that warrants should invariably be secured before arrests are made and that raids should not be conducted without search warrants. The record of the deportation cases under examination raises grave questions as to the propriety of the procedure in this respect.

Affidavit of Probable Cause

The first steps, according to official records, were always taken by special agents of the Department of Justice. Through investigations which they conducted and from so-called confidential sources, they were led to believe that certain aliens advocated the overthrow of the government of the United States by force or violence or were affiliated with an organization which had for its object such a revolutionary purpose. In some cases the arrest occurred before the date of the special agent's affidavit. In the case of Jack Lunee (Warrant No. 54860/784), a telegraphic warrant was issued on January 15, the same day on which Lunee was arrested. The regular warrant was issued on January 17, although the affidavit in the case was dated February 2. Contrary to legal requirement this evidence was seldom forwarded to the proper authorities at Washington and instead of requesting warrants in the usual way they were requested by wire. In many cases the request was made and the warrant was issued by telegram, and later confirmed by mail. This telegraphic request and warrant often included a number of aliens.

Arrests without Warrant

More important than the foregoing is the fact that arrests were frequently made without warrant or even affidavit of probable cause of arrest. The case of Nick Melnick (Warrant No. 54709/349) illustrates this practice. Melnick in his hearing testified that he was walking along Charlton Street, Newark, N. J., about ten o'clock in the evening when he was arrested. In the case of Andrew Lazarowitz (Warrant No. 54709/347) a raid was being made and he paused while passing to learn the cause of the excitement. He was arrested without warrant. John Tarasink (Warrant No. 54709/452) chanced to be in the home of a friend, Tony Chinelli, for whose arrest a police officer had a warrant. Tarasink was arrested without a warrant merely because he happened to be present. A woman, Mary Bunda (Youngstown, Ohio, File No. 2025/392), was taken into custody without a warrant and held for the purpose of securing evidence for the issuance of a warrant which was never issued.

Of our two hundred cases, 89 persons were arrested previously to the issuance of warrants. In 48 cases no date is recorded. Thirteen persons were arrested on the date the warrants were issued, while 47 were arrested after the issuance of the warrant. In one case no warrant was ever issued. In two cases the date of the warrant is not recorded.

The period by which the arrests preceded the issuance of warrants ranged from one to fifty-seven days. George Lapeno (Warrant No. 54860/669) was arrested twelve days before the warrant for his arrest was issued and Peter Kulakowski (Warrant No. 54861/263) was arrested sixteen days before the issuance of his warrant. In the case of Ivan Efimenko (Warrant No. 54861/299) fifty days elapsed between his arrest and the date on which his warrant was issued. In the case of John Ivanauskas (Warrant No. 54861/275) the period was 57 days.

Illustrative Cases

Joe Rodak (Warrant No. 54859/810) was arrested on January 3, 1920, and the warrant was issued six days later. Rodak had lived in the United States eight years and was employed as a car repairer on the N. Y. C. R. R. He had purchased his home on which four hundred dollars was still due. During the war he had registered for the draft and purchased four fifty-dollar Liberty Bonds. Two of these he gave on the property and two he was still paying on at the time of his arrest. When taken into custody Rodak was a member of the Polish Branch of the Socialist Party which by transfer had become a branch of the Communist Party. Rodak stated that he did not know when the change had taken place and did not know the difference between the two organizations. He explained that he had joined the organization because the speakers had told him that the strength of the working man was in the Socialist Party. In support of the charges against the alien no evidence was produced. The warrant was cancelled on April 2, 1920.

The warrant for Peter Kulakowski (Warrant 54861/263) was issued on February 26, 1920, 16 days after his arrest which took place on February 10, 1920. Kulakowski had been in the United States 6 years. He was employed as a coal miner in this country. In Austria he had been a farmer. He registered for the draft and purchased two Liberty Bonds. He was charged with being a member of the Communist Party. This he denied, stating that he was a member of the Ukranian Branch of the Socialist Party at Coal Run, Pa. As evidence of the charge against him a card of membership in the Socialist Party was produced, but no card of membership in the Communist Party was given as evidence.

The Socialist Party at Coal Run merged into the Communist Party. The minutes of a meeting held on November 30th, after this transfer had been made, showed that the alien had been present and had presided. In this connection he stated:

> "I don't know if they kept my name on their books, but I didn't join the Communist Party."

The special agent of the Department of Justice stated that search of the alien's home at the time of arrest yielded nothing of value. When asked during the hearing what reasons he had to offer why he should not be deported, he answered:

> "What can I offer? I did all I could for this country during the war. I worked hard for the Superintendent to have the people buy Liberty Bonds and did everything I could."

The warrant was cancelled April 8, 1920.

John Ivanauskas (Warrant No. 54861/275) was arrested on January 2, 1920. His warrant was not issued until February 28, 1920. Ivanauskas had been in the United States between seven and eight years and had worked for six years as a laborer for the Jewell Clark Stove Works. He registered for the draft, but was put in class five. He purchased two Liberty Bonds and bought war saving stamps to the amount of $5.00. He also contributed to the Red Cross and the Y. M. C. A. As evidence a membership book in the Communist Party bearing the alien's name and address was submitted and also a copy of the Communist Manifesto and other literature said to have been taken from the alien at the time of his arrest. Ivanauskas stated that he had never read the Communist Manifesto or other literature and declared that he did not believe in the use of force or violence, but believed in the United States Government as it is. The testimony further brought out that he did not advocate the overthrow of any government by force and that he did not believe in sabotage, nor subscribe to the principles of Communism. To the direct question as to whether he would be willing to sever connections with the Communist Party if he knew it was against the principles of our Government he replied:

"I renounce right now when it is against the Government."

On April 14th the Assistant Secretary of Labor recommended that the proceedings be stayed for three months. At the end of that time the Inspector-in-charge was instructed to report further on the case.

"Agents Provocateurs"

The term "agent provocateur" has been commonly used to describe a well-known type of official of the czarist regime in Russia. Its meaning is precisely what a transliteration from French into English indicates: "provocative agent." The agent provocateur is employed not merely to apprehend an offender, but to get rid of "undesirables" by inciting them to acts for which they may be apprehended and punished. The practice is so wholly out of repute in this country that no one would publicly offer a justification of it. The Attorney-General has publicly disclaimed the employment of such agents, although it is freely admitted that "under-cover men" are employed by the Department of Justice who mingle freely with radicals and join their organizations. Manifestly the agent must counterfeit radicalism with sufficient accuracy to mislead persons who are experts in that field. To draw the line between the simple agent and the agent provocateur may not be easy. In connection with the raid of January 2, 1920, the Department of Justice issued instructions as follows:

"If possible, you should arrange with your under-cover informants to have meetings of the Communist Party and

Communist Labor Party held on the night set. I have been informed by some of the bureau officers that such arrangements will be made. This, of course, would facilitate the making of the arrests."

A Case in Point

Moreover, the records examined in the present study revealed one case in which the evidence clearly indicated the work of an agent provocateur. This agent appears to have been active in forming local branches of proscribed organizations and in inducing aliens to join them for the purpose of reporting the names to the agents of the Department of Justice. There is no evidence, however, that in so doing he acted on any other than his own initiative.

The case is that of Dyntro Iwankiw (Warrant No. 54860/901). He is an alien, a native of Ukrainia (Russia), thirty-five years of age, who had come to the United States in 1913. Iwankiw had no family and no regular occupation. He had done some writing for radical newspapers, spoke English and acted as an interpreter. His first citizenship papers had been taken out and he had made application for his second papers. Iwankiw had been under arrest three times previously to his being involved in the Communist raids. He was first arrested in Pittsburgh for publishing an article entitled "The Third Revolution in Russia," and a second time in January, 1918, when he was charged with embezzlement. At that time he was released on parole in the custody of the probation officer of Pittsburgh County for a period of two years. He was also charged with running an illicit still in Youngstown. In August, 1919, his third arrest occurred, this time for activities in connection with the Union of Russian Workers. He was found to be a government agent and released.

Iwankiw became an employee of the Amesworthy & Gavitt Detective Agency in Pittsburgh, Pa., in June, 1919, an agency which was furnishing information to the Department of Justice. He was detailed to The Youngstown Sheet and Tube Company, Youngstown, Ohio, "to find out about the activities of the Russian anarchists." There he joined the ranks of the Left Wing of the Socialist Party. On the formation of the Communist Party, he was active in the establishment of the Youngstown local of that organization and was elected its Financial Secretary. Through his activities a number of men were induced to join the local. He kept the Secretary's book concealed in the cellar of his home.

Iwankiw informed an agent of the Department of Justice where the book was kept with the comment that the persons whose names were contained therein "belong to the Communist Party only because of me." According to his testimony, protection was promised him by the Government Agent to whom this information was given. In the event that he was deported he was to receive such documents as would be necessary to re-admit him to the United States. He also stated that he was promised employment with the Department of Justice. The records contain no refutation of these charges.

The testimony of Mr. Amesworthy, of the Amesworthy & Gavitt Detective Agency, showed that he was cognizant of all the facts. He definitely stated in the course of the hearing in this case that this alien, who was a member of the Communist Party, was engaged in getting first-hand information from the general office of that organization in order that this information might be forwarded to the client, who subsequently sent it to the Cleveland office of the Department of Justice. Mr. Amesworthy says:

> "I am in a position to state that the majority of the reports, or at least the greater part of the information contained in all of his reports, were forwarded to Mr. Bliss Morton, Special Agent-in-Charge, United States Department of Justice, Cleveland, by our client."

A Victim of the Agent Provocateur

Raids and a number of arrests were made in Youngstown, Pittsburgh and Cleveland, where Iwankiw was active, solely on the basis of information furnished by this "under-cover man." During the course of this study Alexander Bunda was found to be a victim of the activities of Iwankiw in his capacity as an agent provocateur.

Alexander Bunda (Warrant No. 54860/905) is a native of Galicia, thirty years of age, is married and has two children, both born in the United States, and at the time of this investigation another child was expected. He had been in this country five years and had lived in Youngstown two years, where he worked as a car repairer for the P. & L. E. R. R. He had intended returning to his native country and for that reason had not become an American citizen. In the Spring of 1919 he became a member of the Socialist Party. In the late Fall of that same year he, together with the other members of his branch, were induced by Iwankiw, according to the latter's testimony, as reported in the special memorandum of the Inspector-in-Charge in the Iwankiw case, to transfer to the Communist Party. On or before January 6, 1920, he was arrested, without warrant, on the instigation of Iwankiw.

In his preliminary examination as well as in his subsequent hearings Bunda did not deny membership in the Communist Party, but stated that this membership was by a transfer which, according to his understanding, did not prove him guilty of the charges of anarchy presented in the warrant of arrest. The only evidence submitted in substantiation of the charges against him consisted of a mimeographed copy of page six of the Communist Manifesto and Constitution. Under date of March 27, 1920, the Immigration Inspector-in-Charge of the district submitted a memorandum in which he says:

> "I beg to call attention to the report of the hearing which is being forwarded to-day in the case of Dyntro Iwankiw, who claims that he induced this alien and others to join the Ukranian branch of the Communist Party for the purpose of providing him with information. It is understood that none of the men involved knew that Iwankiw was an 'under-cover' man."

The *New York Times* on January 3rd, in an account of the raids of the preceding night, stated:

> "For months Department of Justice men, dropping all other work, had concentrated on the Reds. Agents quietly infiltrated into the radical ranks, slipped casually into centers of agitation, and went to work, sometimes as cooks in remote mining colonies, sometimes as miners, again as steel workers, and, where the opportunity presented itself, as "agitators" of the wildest type. Although careful not to inspire, suggest, or aid in the advancement of overt acts or propaganda, several of the agents, 'under-cover' men, managed to rise in the radical movement and become, in at least one instance, the recognized leader of a district."

It is due to the Department of Justice to state that this account has been declared false by the Attorney-General's office.

CHAPTER IV

HOW THE ALIENS WERE TRIED

"The Trial"

In the judicial sense there is no "trial" in deportation cases, because the proceeding is wholly administrative. Nevertheless the hearing or examination given to the alien may properly be called, and is commonly called, a trial, since on the determination of fact for which it is conducted depends the destiny of the person involved, and the requirement of fairness is as binding as in a court of justice.

The Interpreter.

Obviously, in the trial of aliens the interpreter is all-important. The records examined in this study raise two grave questions as to the part played by this official.

1. In some cases, as in that of Andrew Chuprina (Warrant No. 54709/551), the indication is that the interpreter's knowledge of English was very slight. A membership book was submitted in the course of the hearing and apparently the alien stated that it was not his.

The following is an exact copy of the dialogue as it appears in the record:

Q. "Whose book is it?"
A. (By the interpreter.) "Same place live with him other fellows. Probably that book belonged to him."
Q. "What were you doing with this book?"
A. (By the interpreter.) "He said he was beaten over there when he was asked the question and he cannot answer. He give him answer that it belonged to him."

The danger involved in putting an accused person at the mercy of this kind of interpreting is obvious.

2. Even more important than the intelligence of the interpreter or his ability properly to interpret the alien's or the inspector's meaning is the question whether the interpreter was in any way connected with the prosecution. In one city where 27 of the 200 arrests reported in this account were made the following facts regarding interpreters were disclosed:

> In 17 of the 27 cases the aliens had an employee of the prosecuting department of the Government as interpreter (Cf. Warrant No. 54811/534).
> In 5 cases the accused spoke English well enough so that no interpreter was employed (Cf. Warrant No. 54809/64).
> In 5 cases the interpreter was not otherwise connected with the case (Cf. Warrant No. 54860/363).

In 3 of the 17 cases in which an employee of the prosecuting department acted also as interpreter, the same man further took the stand simultaneously and testified against the alien. This was true in the case of William Vorinin (Warrant No. 54809/116). In two other cases the interpreter was the man who furnished original affidavit which caused the arrest of the alien, which was introduced as evidence against him (cf. Warrant No. 54859/514 and Warrant No. 54859/492). In another city where 5 of the 200 arrests were made we again find an employee of the prosecuting department of the government acting as interpreter in 4 cases. In the fifth case no interpreter was needed.

Counsel for Alien: The Changed Rule

The counsel for the alien was another important factor in the hearings at which the aliens were asked to prove why they should not be deported. One of the most serious elements in the whole matter under examination is the fact that on December 21, 1919, just prior to the principal raid conducted by the Government, a notable change was made in the rule governing procedure at the hearing given to the alien who is alleged to be unlawfully in the country. The section in question is known as Rule 22, Subdivision 5, paragraph b. Prior to December 31, 1919, the first sentence of this rule read as follows:

> "At the beginning of the hearing under the warrant of arrest the alien shall be allowed to inspect the warrant of arrest and all evidence on which it was issued, and shall be apprised that he may be represented by counsel."

As amended by order of the Acting Secretary of Labor, this sentence reads:

> "Preferably at the beginning of the hearing under the warrant of arrest or at any rate as soon as such hearing has proceeded sufficiently in the development of the facts to protect the Government's interests, the alien shall be allowed to inspect the warrant of arrest and all the evidence on which it was issued and shall be apprised that thereafter he may be represented by counsel."

Delays in Admitting to Counsel

On January 28, 1920, less than a month after this amendment to Rule 22 was promulgated, it was annulled by the Secretary of Labor, and the original form was restored. But in the meantime this obviously important guarantee of the alien's rights was in abeyance and it is impossible to know to what extent injustice was suffered by persons ignorant of the law, knowing English imperfectly and terrified by their sudden seizure and arraignment, in the absence of counsel to aid them in making a defense. So far as the records of the two hundred cases under examination indicate, in no case was the alien informed at the preliminary examination that he was entitled to be represented by counsel at the trial. In some cases this information was not given until the hearing was nearly over.

The records show that 125, or 62.5 per cent of the 200 aliens whose records were examined were represented by counsel at some time during the proceeding, while 71, or 35.5 per cent, for reasons which will be presently stated, waived their right to counsel. In 4 cases the facts relative to such representation were not recorded.

In the case of Prokpey Mojeika (Warrant No. 54860/3) he was not informed of his legal right as to counsel until after nine pages of testimnoy had been taken. At this time alien waived his right to counsel. He was ordered deported. Alex. Bunda (Warrant No. 54860/905) was informed of his right to counsel almost at the very end of his hearing. In the case of Sergy Krook (Warrant No. 54809/344) at the end of the record of hearing we find a note "case deferred for counsel," but there is no record of any further hearing having been held and the alien was ordered deported.

That the alien whose hearing was well under way when he was informed of his right to counsel should waive the right is not surprising. Counsel is not easy to obtain under such circumstances, and after the hearing had "proceeded sufficiently in the development of the facts to protect the Government's interests" the alien in question may very well have considered the advantage of counsel as negligible.

At the same time in some cases other reasons were given for waiving right to counsel, as illustrated in the following:

Alex Grochowski (Warrant No. 54810/191):
"I am ready to defend myself; I don't need any attorney."

Wasil Lalajo (Warrant No. 54709/190):
"I have no money to feed my family, to say nothing of employing an attorney."

Mike Prohorchuk (Warrant No. 54709/167):
"I can talk without counsel."

M. Babiarz (Warrant No. 54859/955) :

"I do not need a lawyer. I have not committed a crime or done anything."

Character of Counsel

The type of the man who acted as counsel for these aliens ranged from the unscrupulous mercenary lawyer to such law firms as Niles, Wolff & Norrow, of which Judge Niles, head of the Baltimore Bar, is senior partner. A representative of the Department of Justice stated in the author's hearing that he had been appointed to act as counsel for one of the aliens.

Types of Evidence Submitted: Photostats

A special study of 124 cases, taken at random, was made with particular reference to the types of evidence submitted in substantiation of the charges of anarchy, etc., made against the aliens. The prevailing form of evidence was found to consist of photostatic copies of various documents such as the Communist Manifesto, Constitution of the Union of Russian Workers, etc. These were made up in stock form and mimeographed and submitted as evidence in 60 cases, or slightly over 48 per cent of the total. In 8 cases no evidence whatsoever was submitted.

Affidavits

In 14 cases the only evidence submitted was the customary affidavit of the Department of Justice. This affidavit also was in a mimeographed form and in substance was a statement that the agent "is informed and verily believes" the alien to be an anarchist or member of a proscribed organization. In some cases the signature of the agent making the affidavit was not affixed. The Record of Preliminary Examination was submitted in 61, or 49 per cent, of the 124 cases examined. In 6 cases it was the only evidence submitted. These records frequently did not bear the signature of the alien or of the officer making the examination and often were extracted under threats and varying forms of compulsion. The absence of the interpreter also gave rise to all kinds of possibilities in the way of misunderstanding, as an examination of the records reveals.

Again, the records of the hearings frequently revealed the fact that the agent making the original charge was asked to produce the evidence or to disclose the source of his information. Invariably he refused to do this.

When questioned concerning his information that the alien was a member of a proscribed organization, the agent would frequently state that his information was derived from confidential sources the disclosure of which he considered would be inimical to the interests of the Government.

Membership Cards

A more substantial type of evidence is found in some cases. In 36 of the 124 cases studied, membership cards were submitted as evidence. Ten of these cards showed membership in the Socialist Party, three membership in the Communist Labor Party, and the remaining indicated membership in one of the proscribed organizations. From some of these it was clear that no dues had been paid to the organizations. Other cards were offered as evidence with no claim that they belonged to the alien, and very few of them bore any mark which would identify them as being the property of the alien.

Other forms of evidence consisted of tickets to meetings and social gatherings given under the auspices of the Socialist or Communist parties; subscription lists containing names of those who had contributed to funds to help the wives of men arrested or for purposes of like character. In the cases of two men there were photographs showing the alien with a copy of a Russian paper called "Bread and Freedom" in his hand. In two other cases, group pictures were submitted purporting to show the members of a local branch of the Communist Party. Post-cards and letters were also frequently found among the exhibits, and when signed "Yours for Communism," were considered particularly strong evidence. (Cf. Jos. Jankauskis, Warrant No. 54860/353.)

A Serious Charge

As an indication of the grave questions raised by the effort to prove a discreditable affiliation the following case may be cited:

Mary Muroff (Warrant No. 54809/987) admitted having been a member of the Communist Party. In her testimony she stated that she did not know that the Communist Party was a proscribed organization and did not know that it advocated force or violence against the United States Government. When told that this was the case she said:

"Had I known that, I would not belong to them."

The examiner asked how she expected him to believe that she knew nothing of the principles of the Communist Party when she had been elected a member of their State Executive Committee. She replied:

"I don't know whether any one will believe me or not, but it is the truth. . . . I don't know the principles; neither have I ever seen their program."

As evidence against her a statement of the Special Agent of the Department of Justice signed by the alien was introduced.

"I signed that, but it says that I signed of my own free will and no force was used to make me sign it, but that is not true. I was compelled to sign it . . . at first I said I did not know whether it would be good for me to sign it, but he said, 'if you do not sign it we will have to go hard on you.' After that was said, I said, 'if that is the case do as you please.' "

She sums up the situation from her point of view when she concludes:

"I have this to say. That if a person belongs to an organization that he does not understand the principles of or its meaning, and thereby makes a mistake, all the facts should be investigated and the benefit given to such a person."

Exceptional Types of Evidence

There were particularly striking types of evidence submitted in various cases, of which the following are examples:

In the case of Fred Poliuk (Warrant No. 54809/800) an interesting piece of evidence was submitted. He was married and had one child and in the six years of his residence in the United States had built up a grocery business which he valued at $6,000 or $7,000. The alien was alleged to have hired a hall for the purpose of holding a radical meeting. Poliuk testified that it was rather for a school for the teaching of English and that the hall had been leased three or four months for this purpose. He was arrested on charges of anarchy on or about January 3, 1920, and after preliminary examination he was released under bond, which he furnished himself to the amount of $1,000. A rather bulky envelop marked "Exhibits" and containing the evidence in the case of this alien was attached to the record of the hearing. When opened, it revealed a bright red flag on which was printed in Russian characters an inscription, the official translation of which was:

"GOOD LUCK TO SOVIET RUSSIA."

No other evidence accompanied this case. Because of the lack of substantial evidence against the alien, on recommendation of the examining inspector and the Commissioner General, in which the Assistant Secretary of Labor concurred, the warrant of arrest was cancelled on April 3rd, three months from the date of his arrest.

In the case of Stanley Dudek (Warrant No. 54859/ 808), the only evidence submitted was a copy of the examination made on the night of his arrest at which the questions had been propounded and answers interpreted by a special agent of the Government. Neither the alien nor the agent were under oath. The defendant did not understand any English whatever. The transcript did not bear the signature of either the alien or the officer making the examination or of witnesses. This and no other evidence was submitted in substantiation of the charges made against the alien. This man was arrested on January 3, 1920, the warrant being issued on January 9th. Bail to the amount of $1,000 was furnished and he was released on or about January 20th. On or about March 22nd, nearly three months after his arrest, the warrant was cancelled.

The case of Joseph Polulech (Warrant No. 54709/ 449) is referred to in another section of this report (Cf. page 60). The only evidence submitted in this case was a carbon copy of extracts from pages 2 and 3 of the membership book of the Union of Russian Workers. No claim was made that the membership book from which these extracts were made belonged to the alien or that it was even found in his possesion, or that it had ever been read by him. This alien was a native of Russia, 27 years of age. He was not married. He had been in this country for 7 years and at the time of his arrest was employed as a packer for the American Distributing Co., 33 Essex Street, New York City. No bail being furnished, Polulech was held in jail from the time of his arrest in November until December 21st, when he was deported on the "Buford."

Change of Charge

In a number of cases where the evidence submitted seemed to be insufficient to prove the charge made against the alien, an additional charge or a change of charge was made.

Andrew Chuprina (Warrant No. 54709/551) is a case in point. Chuprina was born in Russia and was 38 years of age at the time his case was studied. He came to the United States from Winnipeg, Canada, in February, 1916. At the time of his arrest he was living in Detroit with his family, consisting of his wife and three children. He was in the employ of the Western Electric Company. His frugal habits are illustrated by the fact that he had saved several hundred dollars. During the War Chuprina had registered in the Draft, had purchased Liberty Bonds and for ten months he had contributed $1.00 per month toward the support of the Red Cross.

Chuprina was arrested on November 8, 1919, on the charge of being a member of The Union of Russian Workers. The charge was based on the evidence submitted in the case, that the name "Chuprina" occurred in the membership book of the Detroit Branch of The Union of Russian Workers. In the course of the hearing which was held on November 29th, 1919, he definitely and consistently denied the charge of being a member of The Union of Russian Workers, and when the membership book was shown to him it was discovered that only the last name, "Chuprina," occurred, and not his first name. Thereupon the defendant called attention to the fact that there were many Chuprinas living in Detroit, and that he could not be charged with belonging to The Union of Russian Workers.

It was at this point that a new charge was introduced in the case by the examining inspector, who claimed that at the time of entry the alien was liable to become a public charge. An examination of the alien in respect to this point revealed that at the time of entry into the United States he had observed all regulations as to passport, examination by immigration officials, and had at that time $100 in his possession.

Notwithstanding these facts, the inspector conducting the hearing added the following charge to that of anarchy previously made and unsubstantiated:

> "In addition to the charge in the warrant of arrest in this case, I therefore charge that you have been found in the United States in violation of the Immigration Act of February [5], 1917, for the reason that you were at the time of entry liable to become a public charge."

A proceeding of this kind inevitably creates the impression that the official was determined to force the alien out of the country by one means or another.

This alien was ordered deported on December 17, 1919. On June 1, 1920, he was still in jail, having been unable to furnish bond of $10,000 which had been required in his case. On that date the citizens committee of Detroit petitioned the authorities to release the alien on a bond of $500 which they offered to furnish, pending a rehearing in this case. An inspector of the Department of Labor recommended the cancellation of the warrant. The case was ordered reopened on June 11th for a hearing and on September 25th the alien left this country voluntarily.

Statements of Government Agents

Striking also are the testimonies of agents of the Government relative to the evidence submitted in different cases. Frequently the agent made the statement that he was in possession of confidential information the source of which he could not divulge and he could not produce substantial evidence against the alien.

In the case of Jos. Jankauskis (Warrant No. 54860/ 353), the record contains the following question by the inspector and answer by the agent of the Department of Justice:

> Q. "Have you any evidence you desire to offer in this case, or witnesses?"
>
> A. "No, I would like to have the record show the following: Several weeks ago Mr. B. wrote a letter to the Bureau of Immigration giving the names of certain individuals who were recently taken into custody in connection with the radical raids on deportation warrants, for expedient reasons, among them being the inability of the Department and the undesirability of the Department to expose certain confidential informants, the request was made that cases of certain individuals mentioned in such letter be dropped. Among the number is that of this defendant. Pursuant to the representations made in said letter, I am authorized to state here that the Department of Justice has no evidence and there are no witnesses that it cares to introduce in this case."

This alien was arrested prior to February 2, 1920. The warrant of arrest is dated January 12th, but neither the date of arrest nor the date of the preliminary examination is given. The alien was released on bond of $1,000 and on recommendation of the examining inspector and the Bureau of Immigration, in which recommendations the Assistant Secretary concurred, Jankauskis' warrant was cancelled on April 15, 1920, more than two months after his arrest, for lack of substantial evidence.

A statement of similar import is found in the case of Mike Strlhok (Warrant No. 54809/104), in which the special agent states:

> "At the time we applied for the warrant we had ample evidence, secured through confidential sources, that this alien was a member of the Communist Party which, at the present time, I do not believe we are in a position to offer without disclosing

our sources. Therefore, I do not believe we have any evidence at the present time to show in this case. . . . I will further say that the R. Priest from St. Michael came up to the office and told us that he knows the man and that the man probably was a member of the organization, but he went there through some misunderstanding or ignorance and that he is a good church follower. He believes him to be a man of good standing."

Mike Strlhok was arrested prior to January 6th, neither the date of the arrest nor the date of the preliminary examination being given. Bail was furnished and on April 6th, more than three months after his arrest, the warrant was cancelled.

In the case of Wasily Zhestkow (Warrant No. 54859/ 514), the following testimony was given by the agent:

"The file in my possession covering this case discloses no evidence that is competent to introduce here. It is a record of information coming to the Department from apparently creditable confidential sources which indicated in the first instance that this man is connected with one or the other of the outlawed organizations. An investigation has been made concerning him since that time and since his arrest. Such special investigation has failed to disclose anything which justifies the conclusion that he is a bad character or lacks a disposition to be law-abiding. The only thing that appears from the record is his attending of the Soviet Technical School. The only evidence we have, referred to one Elukevich and one Rusak. If the inspector deems it necessary to produce those witnesses here in this case, well and good; otherwise we have nothing further to offer."

This man was arrested on January 2nd. Bail to the amount of $1,000 was furnished and on April 15th, more than three months after his arrest, the warrant was cancelled because of lack of evidence to substantiate the charge.

In the case of Demetri Zosko (Warrant No. 54809/ 128) the agent makes the following statement:

"I would like the record to show this, if you please: That this man was arrested on the basis of his name appearing on a list which we received, apparently authentic. I recognize that fact that this man's name appearing on the list is not positive proof that he is a member, but we concluded it of sufficient account in the first instance for his apprehension subject to such refutation as could be made." [He stated that he had no knowledge of the list except that it had gone to Washington as an official document. When asked if he could have identified the list as an official record, the agent replied that he could not do so "without disclosing confidential informants and under-cover men, and this the Department considers inexpedient."]

This alien was arrested sometime prior to February 3rd, but the date of the arrest and the date of the preliminary examination are not given. On or about January 12th he was released upon the furnishing of bail to the amount of $1,000. On recommendation of the examining inspector and the Bureau of Immigration, in which recommendation the Assistant Secretary concurred, the warrant of arrest was cancelled on April 13th, more than two months after the man's arrest.

Final Disposition

The final disposition of the 200 cases whose records of hearings have been reported herein was as follows:

Warrant cancelled	97
Deportation ordered	78
Proceedings stayed	18
Ordered re-opened	4
Decision pending	1
Released on parole	1
No warrant issued	1
	200

In accord with a provision of the law *habeas corpus* proceedings have been instituted in several cases at the instance of the alien's attorney in order to secure court review of the decision. This action might have been taken in more cases but for the fact that *habeas corpus* proceedings in deportation cases are not usually instituted until the deportation warrant is about to be executed. Relatively few cases have actually reached that stage. Recent decisions in certain cases will be noted in the final chapter.

CHAPTER V

HOW MANY WERE CONNECTED WITH PROSCRIBED ORGANIZATIONS

The Habit of "Belonging"

It is fitting at the beginning of this chapter to indicate how it is often possible for immigrants to belong to objectionable organizations without their being aware of the principles which these societies represent. To a person intimately acquainted with immigrant communities this is not difficult to understand. Immigrants with very little education, such as constitute 90 per cent of every immigrant community, find the main outlet for their social impulses in belonging to all kinds of societies whose number is legion in every immigrant center. They "belong" as naturally and attend as regularly as they eat, not because the organization adheres to one set of principles or to another, but primarily because it is a "society." With nearly every such immigrant society there goes the mutual benefit feature which attracts many. Moreover, it makes an appeal to one's sense of leadership. In one society he is made secretary, in another he may be a teller, but he is an "officer," and that gives him prestige in his community.

It follows that an immigrant frequently belongs to a number of organizations which are contradictory in principles. He may object freely to things said in the meetings but still fail to see the incongruity of his belonging to so many groups differing in objectives or in principles.

As an illustration of this fact the author recalls a conversation with an immigrant whom he knew to be of good antecedents, of fine intelligence and of excellent character. This man had a family of well-bred children, one of whom was attending a university. In conversation one day he revealed the fact that he "belonged" to about ten organizations. There were among them religious societies, some of which were Protestant, some Catholic. One was an association representing Italian national interests, and one was provincial. Another was made up of men who were natives of a small village in Sicily. Among others he spoke of an organization which the author knew to have anarchistic tendencies. Questioned as to why a man in his position belonged to such a group, he shrugged his shoulders and said: "Oh, I go very seldom, and then I go to laugh at them."

A. Classification of Cases

"Proscribed Organizations"

It has already been pointed out that the Secretary of Labor, in accord with his understanding of the Immigration Laws, ruled that membership in the Communist Party was in itself ground for deportation. No ruling was deemed necessary in connection with the Federation of Unions of Russian Workers, which has been considered frankly anarchistic. The I. W. W. and the Communist Labor Party were never thus proscribed.

In addition to persons belonging to these two societies, aliens found to entertain or advocate a belief in the overthrow of the Government of the United States are by the terms of the law liable to deportation. For all practical purposes such persons were on a par with members of proscribed organizations. For this reason instead of making still another class, all persons who were found to be clearly within this deportable group, have been included in the class "members of proscribed organizations."

The two hundred records which form the basis of this study were examined with a view to determining the facts concerning affiliation with the proscribed organizations.   The cases fall into five classes:

FIRST: Those clearly not members of the organizations in question.

SECOND: Those clearly members of a proscribed organization.

THIRD: Those who became members of such organization by automatic transfer.

FOURTH: Students in schools connected with proscribed organizations.

FIFTH: Doubtful cases.

The evidence is so unsubstantial and often so circumstantial that it clearly seemed to have caused perplexity on the part of the inspectors called upon to decide the destiny of the aliens.   In many cases the inspectors appear to have given the benefit of the doubt to the Government rather than to the accused.   They often pronounced judgment against the alien on a pure technicality, and equally as often they made recommendations based upon their personal knowledge of the alien which were inconsistent with their formal judgments.

Four factors have entered into the classification: (1) The evidence submitted at the hearing; (2) testimony given by the alien together with his past record; (3) recommendation made by inspector; (4) the final disposition made in the case of the highest authority in the matter—i.e., the Secretary of Labor.

1. NOT MEMBERS OF PROSCRIBED ORGANIZATIONS

Of the 200 cases here reported 47 belong to this class. They emphatically and in a consistent manner disclaimed connection with such an organization.   Moreover, what was known of their past history, the inconclusiveness of evidence against them, together with the final disposition in their cases, combined to make it clear that these aliens were orderly residents of the United States and in favor of its form of life and government. In many instances they had families in the United States and were desirous of remaining in this country.

A Typical Case.

David Expak (Warrant No. 54810/128) furnishes a typical illustration of this class of alien who clearly did not belong to a proscribed organization.

This alien was a native of Russia, twenty-eight years of age, and had been in this country twelve years. He spoke English, was married and had one child. He and his family lived in Lowell, Mass. He was a cobbler by trade and at the time of his arrest was in business for himself, conducting an establishment in Lowell. The record reveals that he was a man of good standing; he had never been arrested before. He was arrested on or about January 2nd on the charge of being a member of a proscribed organization or believing in the overthrow of organized government. This charge was based upon the affidavit of probable cause made by a government agent stating that this alien's name appeared in the same book as that of one Kulback, and since Kulback was a radical, therefore this alien must be a radical. The affidavit does not state the nature of the book. No evidence was presented in substantiation of the charge of anarchy.

Expak consistently disclaimed membership in any organization whatsoever. In an apologetic manner he even refers to the fact that he is "not a member of any Church because they are far away, one being in Boston and one in Lawrence." The alien did not ask for counsel, but during the hearing a Mr. Edward Tierney testified in his behalf. In the course of the hearing an agent of the Department of Justice stated that this alien should be dismissed because of lack of evidence. In this the Immigration Inspector concurred and finally the warrant was cancelled on April 14, 1920, making the period between the time of arrest and the time of final disposition three and one-half months.

2. MEMBERS OF PROSCRIBED ORGANIZATIONS

Of the 200 cases here reported, 56 were by their own admission or by sufficient evidence submitted, proved to belong to this class. These persons were generally young and unmarried men; they usually acknowledged their membership or anarchistic belief consistently and unequivocally. They made no plea in their own behalf except that they desired to be deported or to be permitted to leave at their own expense.

An Example

The case of Mike Hewes (Warrant No. 54709/991) furnishes illustration, in many respects typical, of aliens belonging to a proscribed organization. Mike Hewes was a native of Galicia, was twenty-eight years of age at the time of his arrest; he was married and had two children born and living in the United States. He had been in America about ten years and at the time of his apprehension was working in a shoe shop in Grand Rapids, Michigan. He had been able to save five hundred dollars. He had secured first citizenship papers six years before and made an attempt to get final papers but had failed to secure them on account of his not speaking English well enough. His father was also living with him and had been in the United States for a year and a half. He also had a brother and a sister in Cleveland. Hewes had registered for the draft but had claimed exemption on account of his having dependents.

He was arrested on or about January 2, 1920, on warrant dated December 27, 1919, on the charge of being a member of the Communist Party. The alien acknowledged having been a member of the Communist Party for about three months. He testified as follows concerning his membership in the Party:

> Q. "Is the Communist Party organized for the purpose of overthrowing the capitalistic Government of America?
> A. "Yes, intended to throw it over. The United States doesn't bother me. I am not a citizen. If I was it would interest me."

The warrant of arrest was read and explained to this alien. Then he was asked whether he understood the charge. To this question he replied:

> "I see the warrant, I believe, but I haven't done any damage yet."

Concerning his deportation he made the following statement:

> "I don't want to go to Galicia because that is under the jurisdiction of Poland and they murder everybody there."

And further:

> "If they deport me I want the wife and children to go with me."
> Q. "Is your wife also a member of the Communist Party?
> A. "When the husband is a member the wife is also. She belongs just like I do."

The alien was unable to furnish bond and was held in detention until March 20, 1920, when order of deportation was issued, and as no deportations to Russia have been effected since that date this alien is still held. (November, 1920.)

It may also be added that Anastasia Hewes, wife of this alien, was also arrested (Warrant No. 54861/127) but proceedings in her case were cancelled.

3. Members by Automatic Transfer

These persons were invariably members of the Left Wing of the Socialist Party. In September, 1919, when the Left Wing formed itself into the Communist Party, many locals were transferred en masse to the Communist Party. The members of these locals were often transferred with their society. In some cases the members had no knowledge of the transfer or did not give their approval thereto; or if they were transferred with their knowledge and approval of transfer they appear to have had no knowledge of the significance of the transfer or of any illegal principles which the organization was alleged to embrace.

It sometimes happened that the alien had paid dues for a year in advance in the Socialist Party. After the transfer from the Socialist to the Communist Party these dues were applied to the latter, thus technically bringing the alien into the proscribed class whether or not he approved of his transfer. The final decision in the matter seemed to have depended upon a referendum vote of each local branch. The question of membership of such cases in the proscribed classes is very doubtful.

Attention may also be called to the fact that these persons became members by the automatic transfer of an organization long before the organization was declared proscribed by the authority of the Secretary of Labor. When the organization became proscribed they did not have an opportunity to declare themselves in favor of or against the outlawed organization. Of the 200, 74 became members of one of the proscribed organizations in this manner. Of these 29 were entirely ignorant of the transfer, while 45, although having a knowledge of the transfer, seemed not to understand its significance.

Transfer Without Alien's Knowledge

A typical example of this class is furnished by the case of Paul Rosensky (Warrant No. 54811/603). Paul

Rosensky was a Lithuanian, thirty-one years of age. He was single and at the time of his arrest he had been in this country six years. He was in the employ of the Illinois Central Shops, Burnside, Illinois. An interpreter was used in his case. He had served in the Russian Army and had registered for the draft during the recent war and was placed in class five. He had a step-brother living in this country with him. He had first citizenship papers.

He was arrested at his home on or about January 2, 1920, on warrant of the same date, charging him as being a member of the Communist Party. He was given a regular hearing on January 31, 1920, and was ordered to be released on bond.

When questioned as to his organization membership he testified as follows:

"I was a member of the Socialist Party, and they told us to change our name and I remained Secretary."

A considerable amount of evidence was submitted in this case which consisted of the usual quotation from the Manifesto and Program of the Communist Party; a card showing membership in the Communist Party; a charter of the party together with the minutes book of the branch kept by Rosensky himself. There was also submitted the official stamp of the Communist Party, together with a suitcase belonging to the alien containing Communist books, etc.

The alien did not deny that he was a member of the Communist Party but stated that he had paid dues a year in advance in the Socialist Party and that this made him, *ipso facto,* a member of the Communist Party. He testified further that his local branch had protested against affiliation with the Communist Party:

Q. "Did the members of your local ever vote as a local to affiliate with the Communist Party of America?"

A. "No, we were protesting all the time."

Q. "Did your local take part in the referendum vote on the question of joining the Communist Party with other locals of the Lithuanian Socialist Federation?"

A. "Yes."

Q. "Do you know what the result of the referendum was?"

A. "I don't know."

Q. "Has any official notice been served upon you or any other member of your local as to what the result of that referendum was?"

A. "We don't know yet."

Q. "Did your local No. 137 of the Lithuanian Socialist Federation ever vote to apply for a charter in the Lithuanian Communist Federation?"

A. "No. . . . As soon as we find out the result of the referendum why we may remain in the Socialist Party or the majority of the members will vote to come back in the Socialist Party."

Q. "Was membership in local No. 137 open to the public?"

A. "Yes, but since we changed the name we did not invite anybody to become a member because we did not know to what party he belonged."

As to his attitude toward the government of the United States the alien gives the following rather hazy expression:

Q. "Do you believe in a change in the Government in any way?"

A. "I am not an American citizen and I don't think about and I am not engaged in it. I have nothing against the Government."

A summary of findings as well as the final disposition makes this case a typical example of this class. On April 16th order was given as follows: Stay proceedings three months; Inspector-in-Charge to be instructed to report at end of that period.

Transfer Not Understood by Alien

The case of Elia Matushko (Warrant No. 54859/464) furnishes a typical illustration of aliens who were transferred from the Left Wing of the Socialist Party to the

Communist Party with knowledge of the transfer but without knowledge of the significance of the transfer.

Matushko was a Russian twenty-five years of age. At the time of his arrest he had been in this country eight years. In Russia he had lived on a farm; in this country he was working in a cafeteria in Chicago. He was single. He had never been arrested before. He could read and write in his own language, but it is not clear whether he could speak English; an interpreter was employed in his case. He had registered for the draft and had been placed in class five. He was arrested on or about January 7, 1920, and apparently was held in the House of Correction, where he was given a regular hearing on January 15, 1920.

When informed as to his right to counsel he said:

"I have not got anything. I didn't commit any crime. I don't need any lawyer."

When questioned on the point he frankly admitted both activity and membership. The following is from his testimony:

"I joined the Socialist Party. My desire was to get an education and there was a school at this branch of the Socialist Party and I joined it. When I started to attend this school they told me I joined the Socialist Party and then the Socialist Party was transformed into the Communist Party. I didn't know the particulars or the reason this thing was done, but I find out later on we are members of the Communist Party. I didn't hear the principles of this organization up to this morning. It is the first time I heard about the program. Part of it I heard, but not all of it. The important part I did not hear until this morning."

Regarding his attitude toward the Government of the United States the alien testified:

"I have nothing to do with this country. I am not a citizen of this country. I absolutely do not believe in any change of government in this country. My country is Russia and I am a citizen of Russia, and that is why I am concerned in it."

Matushko expressed his desire to be deported to his native country. Therefore, on April 13th he was ordered deported "solely for membership in the Communist Party." He has thus far (November, 1920) not been deported.

4. STUDENTS IN SCHOOLS CONDUCTED BY OR IN CONNECTION WITH RADICAL ORGANIZATIONS

Of our 200 cases 8 were arrested and detained because or as a result of their being connected with schools maintained by or in connection with radical organizations. Examples of such schools were those conducted in the People's House in New York City, and the House of the Masses in Detroit. From the records it does not appear that these young men were strictly members of any of the proscribed organizations. It may be, however, that radical instruction was being given at these schools although the records mentioned only English, history, civics, arithmetic, engineering, automobiling and Russian as the major subjects taught.

Joseph Polulech (Warrant No. 54709/449) furnishes a clear example of this type. Polulech was a Russian, twenty-seven years of age, single, and had come to the United States in 1912. At the time of his arrest he was in the employ of The American Distributing Company, 33 Essex Street, New York City. He was attending a school conducted in the building known as the People's House on 15th Street in New York City. On the evening of November 7, 1919, while taking a lesson in mathematics he was arrested without warrant. The record of the hearing did not include the affidavit of probable cause and there is no indication that the alien had even the customary preliminary examination upon being arrested. No evidence was offered by the authorities in substantiation of the charge that the alien was an objectionable person except that in the course of the hearing a mimeographed copy of pages two and three of the membership book of The Union of Russian Workers were read in the record, but it was not even claimed that this membership book had been read by or belonged to or had been found in the possession of the alien.

A hearing was given Polulech on November 9th, and on November 25th before an immigrant inspector at Ellis Island. In answer to the question whether he desired to be represented by counsel the alien stated:

> "I cannot tell anything more to a lawyer or through a lawyer than I can tell to you. I am ready to answer all questions."

Belonged Only to the Church

In answer to the various questions the alien in a consistent and straightforward, positive manner testified that he was not a Communist, and that he was not a member of any proscribed organization and that the only organization to which he belonged in the United States was the Methodist Episcopal Church on Second Avenue, New York City. He declared:

> "I am not an anarchist, I do not belong to anything but the Church."

Aside from an examination of the official record of the trial of this alien a careful inquiry was made of his pastor concerning his character and conduct. It was learned that Mr. Polulech, who was a member of his Church, was ambitious, orderly, and a well-behaved young man. He became a member of the Church in 1913 and had been up to the time of his arrest a constant attendant and an active worker. Only two evenings before his arrest he had attended a meeting of the Brotherhood, of which he was an officer. He was also a constant attendant of the evening classes conducted by the

Church, and especially interested in American history, civics, and the English and Russian languages. When, in 1919, the Church was unable to open its usual evening classes on account of insufficient funds, Polulech began attending classes at the People's House.

Mr. Polulech had favored the United States form of government but had kept his Russian citizenship on account of the fact that he desired to return to Russia as an educational missionary for the uplift of his people. During the war he had been an active member of Liberty Loan Committees and had made substantial contributions to every war cause as well as to the maintenance of the Church and its activities.

The pastor and other friends of Mr. Polulech were astounded at his being arrested, but were unable to come to his rescue. It seems that he wrote daily letters from Ellis Island to his friends and especially to his pastor. Some of these letters were not received and likewise it appears that some of the letters that his pastor and friends wrote him were not received by him.

At the second hearing Polulech, when asked the same questions which had been propounded at the first hearing, refused to answer, as a protest, in which he was joined by others, against the practice of interposing a screen between the prisoners and their friends who came to see them. He claims that the authorities had broken their promise to correct this practice.

Before he could establish connections with friends who would gladly have helped him, Polulech was deported on December 21, 1919, after having been held in custody and "incommunicado" for six weeks.

5. DOUBTFUL CASES

The fifth class is made up principally of persons who seem to have had some tendency toward radicalism and who at some time were definitely connected with one of the proscribed organizations. These aliens generally acknowledge previous membership but definitely denied being members of the proscribed classes at the time of arrest. No effort was made or evidence submitted by the authorities to prove that such was the case.

Of the 200 cases here reported 15 fall within this class. Two of these were ordered deported, three were held pending further hearing, ten were either dismissed on cancellation of the warrant or released on their own recognizance.

A Polish Patriot

The case of R. Mitchell (Warrant No. 54709/163) furnishes a typical example of this class. Mitchell was a native of Poland, was twenty-five years of age and had been in the United States five years. He was single. He had lost one arm while working for the American Brass Company at Ansonia, Conn. He could read and write in the Russian and Polish languages. He had studied English and could understand it very well but could not speak fluently. During the war he had registered in the draft, had waived exemption and was placed in Class A for limited service. He had also made contributions to the Red Cross and various other war funds and had bought War Savings Stamps. His reason for not being a citizen of the United States he stated thus:

"I am a Polish Patriot and all my lifetime I dreamt of Polish independence. I read in the papers that perhaps in three months, perhaps six months, the war will be ended and the way will be made clear for me to go back to my native land. That is why I did not make any effort to become a citizen of the United States."

Mitchell was arrested on or about November 7, 1919 on warrant dated November 6, 1919 by local police on a charge of being a member of the Union of Russian Workers. He was given a regular hearing on November 21, 1919, and a second hearing on November 26, 1919. Bail was asked in the first instance in the amount of one thousand dollars and later raised to twenty-five hundred dollars.

The statement was made by the special agent that he had in his possession evidence against this alien consisting of a number of books, pamphlets and correspondence, including a letter addressed to the alien by the State Secretary of the Communist Party in Connecticut, inviting him to the State Convention of the Communist Party at New Haven, September 28, 1919. Another letter was said to have been written by the alien to a person in New Britain, Conn., directing him to use his influence in the interest of revolutionary socialism. The letters pertained to meetings and other business regarding the organization. A copy of the preliminary examination contained the statement that the alien had admitted that the Polish Society to which he belonged had become a part of the Communist Party and that he was a member but had the right to resign if not in accord with its principles.

Regarding this statement the alien gives the following testimony:

A. "I am not sure as to the nature of his questions, as he talked to me in English. I remember distinctly one question that I wanted to answer him and I said 'talk to me in Polish.' He refused to talk to me in Polish.

Q. "Was an interpreter present during the questioning?

A. "I don't know whether he had an interpreter with him or not. There was no interpreter to translate questions to me in Polish and I asked him to talk to me in Polish.

In the particular case of Mitchell the main exhibits claimed to have been submitted in the original case were absent and no record of their ever having actually been submitted, was found.

Regarding his belief in anarchy the alien made the following statement:

"I will say, relative to the warrant, that I am not an anarchist. I consider myself an enemy to anarchism. I belong only to the Polish section of the Socialist Party. What the warrant says, that I do not believe in organized government, is not true. I believe in organized government. I consider myself a friend of the United States and therefore I am throwing away such a charge. During the time of the war I worked for the United States in the American Brass Company. The following, for example: During the registration, in the questionnaire I stated that the Government could have me at once if they want me, and they put me in the first class A—for limited service."

He gave further expression to his belief:

Q. "What statement have you to make particularly to the charge in the warrant that you are a member of or affiliated with an organization that teaches disbelief in all organized government?

A. "My organization does not teach this belief. My organization has its newspaper, 'Glos Robotniczy,' which has postal permission and therefore I read the articles. I do not find them dangerous for the American Government, because it is freely permitted for circulation."

He further states:

"I am a Christian and have nothing against God."

In view of the fact that this alien claimed to be a Polish patriot and the fact that the American people have always stood for the protection of such patriots the case was deemed doubtful. At the time our investigator visited Hartford County Jail this alien was still detained. The warrant had been cancelled January 6, 1920.

B. Motives Prompting Affiliation with Proscribed Organizations

The aliens' motives as stated by themselves, for joining various organizations and their interpretation of the principles of their societies also constitute an interesting and fruitful inquiry. The aliens who admitted membership in proscribed organizations gave various reasons for their affiliation. These reasons may be roughly classified as educational, economic, social and political.

Educational Aims

By far the greater number give as their reason for belonging to a proscribed organization their desire for knowledge of one kind or another. The following cases are typical:

John Huacuk (Warrant No. 54859/830) said that he joined to:

> "Learn to read and write arithmetic."

Alexander Kuchinsky (Warrant No. 54861/9) said:

> "I desire to learn about automobiles. I discovered that those who knew how to repair automobiles and run them make good pay and I wanted to do so."

William Vorinin (Warrant No. 54809/116) gave as his reason:

> "As a lover of music I joined this organization (Socialist Party); when I was in the chorus I was told I must belong to the organization and so I joined."

R. Mitchell (Warrant No. 54709/163) stated:

> "I entered the party for the reason that I could learn the history of the Polish workers and the history of mankind and, therefore, I strived to read, though not much, but all that was done by the Socialist Comrade Dashinsky and his party in my native land, Poland."

Political Motives

There were some who belonged to the organization for political reasons, declaring their political interest to be confined to Russian politics.

Sam Kot (Warrant No. 54860/787) gave as his motive:

"I am a Soviet citizen. As you know my wife and children are there and I joined an organization because I want to be met by the Soviet Government of Russia as a citizen."

Maxim Bazeluk (Warrant No. 54860/385) states:

"I was told that the Russian people were working for Russia but not against America. I thought that when they were agitating that they were agitating only about Russia but did not say anything about America."

Peter Falkowsky (Warrant No. 54709/762) said:

"I am only learning about the Communist Party so as to be ready when I get back to Russia not to be a fool when I get there."

One man—Feodor Semenchuk (Warrant No. 54860/-596)—understood that he could only return to Russia by becoming a member of the Communist Party.

Economic Reasons

Some of the aliens had an idea of improving their economic status by joining the organization in question. One instance will suffice.

Michael Babiarz (Warrant No. 54859/955) said that he:

"Joined because speakers said that the capitalists keep the working men down and try to get them to work as cheaply as possible and that it was time for the laboring man to organize for the purpose of getting better conditions and better pay."

Social Aims

Still others joined these organizations purely for social reasons as a large number of immigrants in this country are wont to do.

Joe Rive (Warrant No. 54811/946) accounts for his membership as follows:

"I would be able to send home money and correspond with my mother and brothers. The man also told me they have music and singing and that I could pass a pleasant evening."

Peter Baker (Warrant No. 54809/300) testifies:

"I don't know what it means but I have been a member

for three months. I didn't sign anything. All I did I don't know what it was, but I now realize what is going to happen to me. The only thing I joined for was to pass my time."

Tony Vasilewich (Warrant No. 54709/443) had an understanding that the organization to which he belonged was a sick benefit society. He states:

"When I joined this organization, Union of Russian Workers, I thought it was a mutual benefit society and after getting acquainted with them on one occasion I asked them if they give sick benefit, and they laughed at me and I quit them."

Gabriel Romanovich (Warrant No. 54709/462) gives the same reason:

"The purpose of it is first to help each other in case of sickness."

C. ALIENS' INTERPRETATION OF THE PURPOSE OF THESE ORGANIZATIONS

The alien was rarely asked or offered an opportunity to state what was his understanding of the purpose of the organization of which he was charged with being a member. In a few cases, however, voluntary expression was given by the alien himself concerning his understanding of the purpose of the organization. Following are a few citations of such expressions:

1. FEDERATION OF UNIONS OF RUSSIAN WORKERS

Nickoli Gorin (Warrant No. 54861/145) said:

"It is an organization for teaching culture and education."

Michael Sawicki (Warrant No. 54709/348) said:

"A Union for the purpose of teaching illiterate people by blackboards."

Nicholas Melnicoff (Warrant No. 54861/306) gave the following interpretation:

"As I understand they are helping the laborers, those who are in need and out of work, they are helping each other."

Nicholas Steczyzyn (Warrant No. 54734/229) had a somewhat different understanding:

> "My idea would be to agitate, educate and organize and get so strong that we could step in and take control of everything without bloodshed or at least with a very small amount of it."

Christopher Hetaguroff (Warrant No. 54861/48) understood the purpose as being:

> "Brotherhood, equality and truth."

2. COMMUNIST PARTY

Sam Merkowich (Warrant No. 54859/159) gave this as the purpose of the Communist Party:

> "Stands for the workers' control; industrial democracy or political democracy, what we call it. To get control of Government they will organize a majority of the workers through parliaments and when they have a majority of the workers organized, take the reins of Government."
> Q. "Do you mean get control of the ballot?"
> A. "Yes."

In the minds of some the purpose bordered on political aims, mainly dealing with conditions in Russia.

Alex. Pawlukovich (Warrant No. 54860/216) said:

> "I understand that the principles of the Communist Party are invoked by the working class of the entire world. If the working class of this country want to make a violent change or a peaceful change it is their business."

Nicholas Torbiak (Warrant No. 54861/261) outlined his understanding in the following words:

> "You see, we recognize in Communism to not have in our country kings like there were there, because we were suffering under kings. We were just used like animals. Lots of our boys had to leave their country and go find some place else to make their living, like me, I came to the United States. I was making my living in the United States and you see that is why the people decided in the old country to have a

Communist Party and have the communists control the country instead of kings or czars, because czars used us like animals."

Catherine Bloom (Warrant No. 54861/120), a native of Holland, made an interesting statement at the hearing. She had no interpreter and seemed to be a thoughtful and well informed woman. She gave her occupation as housewife and we were able to learn that her husband was not arrested and had furnished bail for her release. They owned their own home and seemed to be in fairly good financial circumstances. She stated that she had purchased one fifty dollar Liberty Bond and added:

"I wanted to be naturalized so that I could vote, but they would not take me."

She was Treasurer of her branch of the Communist Party at the time of her arrest. This branch had formerly been a part of the Socialist Party. In explaining the transfer she said:

"The only reason we left the Socialist Party, we did not believe in using the working people's money for elections and the outcome of elections."

She distinctly stated that she did not believe in the use of force or violence but strongly advocated changes by means of education.

"I believe, if we would educate these people to that point, they would become citizens as soon as they saw it was agreeable."

Mrs. Bloom definitely wished to remain in this country.

Julius Ohsis (Warrant No. 54859/581) said:

"In our organizations nothing has been said about these statements in the warrant about the overthrow of the Government of the United States. I have never heard discussed anything as they have in the warrant about using force or violence in overthrowing the Government of the United States."

Peter Baker (Warrant No. 54809/300) had a social understanding:

"As I understand it, it was just to get together to enjoy the evenings because there was no other place to go."

Nick Saloff (Warrant No. 54861/31) said:

"I wanted to belong for the purpose of enlightment and discussion."

Demetri Zosko (Warrant No. 54809/128) understood the organization as having an economic purpose:

"This organization represented the workers and give them a better chance to obtain a better living, and me, being a family man, naturally I joined them."

CHAPTER VI

HOW THE ALIENS FELT ABOUT LEAVING AMERICA

Interesting also is the attitude of the aliens toward deportation. The simplicity of the testimonies give them weight and indicate whether or not these men were really against America or the United States Government. In this respect the study of the records reveals three distinct types:

(1) Those who clearly expressed their desire to remain in the United States. These for the most part had families in this country and were not connected with any proscribed organization.

(2) Those who expressed a desire to leave this country either at their own expense or by deportation. These in the main belonged to the proscribed classes and were generally unmarried or men who had families in Europe. Some of them also stated unequivocally that they had made an attempt to secure proper passports to leave this country but had failed.

(3) Between these two types there were a number of persons who were indifferent as to deportation. The circumstances of their arrest and prosecution seem to have operated to render them passive on the subject of their fate.

Of our 200 records 82 throw no light on this subject. Of the remaining 118, 45 definitely stated that they desired to remain in this country; 50 wished to leave, and 21 were entirely indifferent.

The following are typical expressions of preference, on the part of the aliens, as taken from the records.

A. Those Wishing to Remain in the United States

Fred Stebler (Warrant No. 54859/670):

"I want to be a citizen and I want to stay here because my family is here."

Peter Baker (Warrant No. 54809/300):

"The only thing I can say is that I like this country and would like to live here."

R. Sieman (Warrant No. 54810/1):

"I will learn to read and write, get my papers and be a citizen, work hard and get an education for my children and family—that is all. . . . I tell you that I thirteen years in this country, and I never done anything; I worked hard during the war, seven days a week, twelve hours a day; I bought Liberty Bonds, gave to the Red Cross; I gave to soldier funds, bought Thrift Stamps; now, I pray, let me have liberty."

Gospodin Grozeff (Warrant No. 54709/846) (a Bulgarian):

"My wife is from England. It is a hard thing for her to go to Bulgaria, as she cannot speak the language. If they let me stay in this country I will be a citizen of the United States."

Harry Bratok (Warrant No. 54860/917):

"I like American laws and I thought I would die here."

B. Those Desiring to Leave the United States

Alex. Pawlukovich (Warrant No. 54860/216):

"I want to go of my own free will and in any case I would like to go soon."

Joe Koza (Warrant No. 54709/342):

"If the United States Government wished to deport us, help us cross the border and we will go ourselves. . . . I would be favored."

Nick Saloff (Warrant No. 54861/31):

"If I can go out to work now and the Russians are then permitted to leave this country, I will go back right away when I get money enough."

Frank Kuneskis (Warrant No. 54860/930):

"Don't want to be sent out by the United States Government. Let him give us time and we will go back ourselves. Don't want to be sent back like cattle."

Some of these aliens made a definite effort to secure passports to leave this country:

Wasily Wasilewicz (Warrant No. 54860/333):

"There was no one to issue passports unless it be Bachmetieff, who could issue me a passport to eastern Siberia, where the Japanese are, and I did not want to go there. . . . I do not wish and do not ask for any favors. I want to be released since I am not guilty of any crime and be permitted to arrange my travel matters myself."

Nikolai Koropotko (Warrant No. 54709/345):

"I want to go back because the American Government showed it did not want me here. First, they refused to give me papers* when I applied for them. Second, they arrest me and keep me here three weeks without reason, so I want to go back to Russia so not to be in the way of the United States Government."

C. Those Who Were Indifferent to Deportation

Jack Gaidis (Warrant No. 54859/866):

"Whatever you want to do with me is all right."

Dimitry Babruk (Warrant No. 54810/845):

"If they want to deport me, let them deport me."

Martin Svezda (Warrant No. 54860/919):

"I have nothing to say. If you want to send me, go ahead and send me."

Jerto Jenkovich (Warrant No. 54861/319):

"If the Government believes I should not be here and that I am not fit to be here, then it is up to them; what they decide."

Vincent Martzin (Warrant No. 54709/276):

"If I am considered not guilty, I wish to be released, and if guilty, I am ready to be deported. I wish my family to accompany me."

* The reference here is probably to a futile application for passports.

Ephrim Zolotum (Warrant No. 54860/415) :

"Personally, I do not feel guilty of any charge, but if the Government finds me dangerous to live in this country, they may deport me."

Elarton F. Shelig (Warrant No. 54861/147) :

"I did not do anything; if they find it is necessary to deport me because I am not an American citizen they can do anything they wish to me."

"Americanization"

No more illuminating statement bearing on these aliens' attitude toward America, appears in the whole series of records studied than the words of the Polish alien, Tony Smollok (Warrant No. 54709/280) :

"When I came to this country, and saw the Statue of Liberty, I tipped my hat to it and I was happy. During my stay in this country, I could not find any understanding from the American people towards myself, and have been frowned upon all the time as a 'Polack' in public places. When my wife came here, both of us went to work, and my wife also came to the conclusion that Americans did not treat her as they treated one another, but always called her 'Polack.' The final result is that the wife is in the hospital and I am arrested by the government which I tried to understand and obey."

Attitude toward America

The interviews held in prisons revealed the attitude of the aliens toward America, and the degree to which they had become absorbed into our national life. At the Hartford County Jail when the prisoners were asked whether they desired to remain in the United States or to return to Europe, sixteen men expressed the desire to stay in this country and forty wanted to return to Europe. The others who answered the question were indifferent as to whether they stayed here or went back to Europe. One of the men who wished to stay in this country was thirty-six years of age and had been in America for eight years. He had received a letter from

his wife stating that she had started for the United
States. He wished to be released in order that he might
meet her. This man admitted being a philosophical anarchist. Another man, a printer, married, with four
children, who had been in this country for fifteen years,
said that he wished to remain in this country unless he
could be deported with his wife and children. He had
been arrested on February 6th. He said that on the very
day on which the prison was visited, Thursday, March
25, he had received a letter from his wife in which she
stated that she had given bail on the previous Monday.
He did not understand why he had not been released.
One of the men who desired to return to Russia wanted
to be released long enough to earn money with which
to go. He wanted to pay his own way. In Youngstown,
Ohio, on the other hand, none of the prisoners wished
to leave America. Twelve definitely preferred to remain
here, at least for a time, provided they could be freed.
One man said he wished to stay if he could "work in
peace"; two seemed indifferent, and one made no reply
to the question.

Interviews with the Detroit prisoners did not reveal
clearly whether they preferred to stay in the United
States or not. Many, however, indicated a desire to be
freed and if they had to go they would go voluntarily
and at their own expense. In general, however, these
men showed a more arrogant attitude toward America.
Repeatedly they stated that they had met many bad, but
no good, Americans. Said one of them, "If money in
pocket Americans like you, if not, don't care or swear at
you." A common complaint was: "Here they want only
money." Several of the men, however, had been impressed by Americans whose acquaintance they had made
in the labor union or elsewhere.

CHAPTER VII

HOW THE ALIENS WERE TREATED

A. Treatment at Time of Arrest and Preliminary Examination

Attention has already been called to the fact that out of the two hundred cases reported in this account ninety-one of the aliens were arrested without warrant. The records unquestionably disclose rough treatment at the time of arrest. Seventeen men distinctly testified at the hearings that they were pounded with clubs, black jacks, hand-cuffs or were threatened into submissiveness at the point of a revolver, either at the time of arrest or in the course of the preliminary examination.

Personal Testimony

The following quotations indicate the treatment alleged by some of the aliens to have been received by them at the time of arrest:

E. Beriezovski (Warrant No. 54809/7):

"Instead of showing me a warrant they showed me a black jack and a revolver."

Afanasi Slawetski (Warrant No. 54860/260):

"Nothing was shown me at that time until they showed me their revolvers and told me to put my hands up and searched my pockets and handed whatever they found from one to another."

Necita Zafronia (Warrant No. 54709/284):

"I have lived long enough in Russia, under the Czar. I have seen brutality committed there, but I have never seen the brutality that was committed on the Russian people here. In my case, when I was arrested, four men came into the room in the evening, when I was partly undressed, and was doing exercises in arithmetic, and asked my name and told me to go along with them. They showed me a badge, but did not tell me the reason for my arrest. When I left the house and at the time I was travelling in an automobile, they were beating me in the sides with their hand-cuffs and this continued all the way until they brought me to the Park Row Building in New York. In a room where they took me and asked me my name they were beating me again, without any explanations."

In a number of cases we find reference to threats and similar treatment given the alien in the course of the preliminary examination for the apparent purpose of extracting evidence from him.

John Cherniawsky (Warrant No. 54709/465) in the course of the hearing made the following statement:

A. "I stay in police station about four days after; four days they come and ask me over at the police station. They ask me into another room, and they ask what about this book, and say stand up, this side of the wall, and they say I am going to shoot you. Nobody go. Somebody said to pull the curtains down and Mr. A. there say to shoot him down and they didn't pull the curtains down. They only felt on the side. Another fellow take this gun and say, I am going to shoot you, and he said, tell the truth, and I said, what I told I am saying is the truth, and he pulled down that gun and started to slap me in the face and this fellow take [and] grab me in the neck."

Q. "You mean Mr. A. grabbed you by the neck?"
A. "This fellow."
Q. "That is Mr. A.?"
A. "Yes, and another fellow—I think fellow that arrested first time in the hall—I don't know what his name—white collar, he slapped too. I know very well W———, that is the name."
Q. "Now, did anything else happen?"
A. "That is all."

B. TREATMENT IN JAILS AND DETENTION STATIONS

Since the records examined consist of hearings given the aliens in the first part of their period of detention they contain no evidence relative to the treatment of the prisoners while detained in jail. A personal investigation made at the prisons, however, supplies evidence of interest and importance on the subject. At Pittsburgh and Youngstown conditions were found to be relatively good. But both at Hartford and at Detroit a serious situation was found to have existed, which must be briefly described.

I. Hartford, Conn., County Jail, February 28, 1920

The Prison Cells

The part of the jail in which the aliens were held is made up of a series of individual cells arranged in the form of a rectangle. Each row of cells forms a tier in a deck-like structure. Each floor or desk supports a tier of twenty-five cells. The barred side of each cell opened into a corridor about two and one-half feet wide. Each man was held in one of these cells with no opportunity for direct communication with the others.

At the end of each tier there were three cells, or six cells in each tier, in which, on account of the concentration of steam pipes in the corridor, the air was hot and suffocating. The men in these cells were naked or nearly so when the cells were inspected. They complained bitterly of not having sufficient air and some appeared very listless. Three of the men said that if they were held much longer under such conditions, they would die of consumption. The attention of a prison officer was called to this state of things. It was pointed out to him that there were some vacant cells in the middle of each tier where the air was better and the question was asked whether the men might not be transferred to these cells. The officer stated that it would involve too much trouble and red tape and would not be worth while.

Held "Incommunicado"

The prisoners were asked a number of general questions. They seemed to be very eager for news and upon inquiry it was discovered that they had been held "incommunicado." They had not seen a newspaper, English or otherwise, nor had they received letters from their relatives or friends. They had not been permitted visits from their friends until the latter part of January. A conversation was heard between a prison officer and one of the aliens who was known as the "Professor." This man was desirous of sending a note to his wife, who was waiting outside. The officer refused to grant the permission, stating that he could only send her his address.

In the office of one of the departments of the government, a number of letters were seen on a desk addressed to the men in the jail. One of them bore the January postmark, and was therefore at least a month old. They were open and arranged in tiers with elastic bands around them. An officer informed the investigator that the letters were being held for censorship.

While the investigator was in the same office, three persons came in to ask permission to interview the prisoners. In each case there was considerable argument and pleading before the permission was granted. A woman with a little child of about seven years of age, pleaded at length for permission to visit her husband. Outside of the same office a woman was seen with a suitcase of food and clothing. When questioned she stated that her brother had been in jail for a month and that she had not been permitted to see him. A permit was finally granted her and she was very much pleased.

On a later visit—March 25th, 1920—other persons were found to be held incommunicado.

Fourteen men were in the upper cells. No interview with these men was allowed because they had not had their first hearing and therefore were held incommunicado. According to records, they had been in prison since March 11, or two weeks. On April 2, eight days later, they still had not had their first hearing and were still held incommunicado. In other words, these fourteen men were held for three weeks without hearing and without a knowledge on the part of the authorities as to whether or not they were members of a proscribed organization.

II. Detroit Prison (Fort Wayne), April 9-10, 1920

On April 9 and 10 a similar investigation was made of the aliens held in custody at Detroit in the Wayne County Jail on charges of anarchy and similar beliefs. There were at the time about 150 men being held in detention, all of whom had been seized in raids. There was no complete record of the total number of prisoners who had been held. Eighty-two men were interrogated.

The "Black Hole"

The conditions surrounding the imprisonment of these men were exceedingly bad at first. Since no adequate quarters were available for the large number of prisoners taken in Detroit and vicinity, the upper floors of the Post Office building were converted into a prison in which hundreds of men were held. A prominent citizen of Detroit compared the situation with the Black Hole of Calcutta. The conditions became so bad that the Mayor of the city protested, not on the ground of justice to the prisoners, but because of menace to the health of the city which this situation created. Finally the Federal Barracks at Fort Wayne were secured and the aliens were transferred to them.

Rough Treatment

A Government representative at Detroit stated that when he first took over the situation, there had been a considerable amount of graft among the guards who were surrounding the men and who, for the most part, were uneducated men who used profanity freely and who, having little sympathy with the prisoners, gave them abusive treatment. Two men seemed to have escaped from the Barracks and on account of this, severe punishment was inflicted on the prisoners who in turn went on a hunger strike in order to bring about a change in the treatment. This strike continued for two days without serious results. The prisoners, however, were refused permission to receive relatives and friends after that for a period, but at the time of the investigation, the prisoners were doing their work steadily and were being allowed an hour out of doors in good weather—sometimes two hours.

Sickness

The food given the prisoners was good, but the congestion which they suffered during the first days of their imprisonment, made several of them seriously sick. Although the men were left without care, which endangered the health of the entire number, there were no serious results.

CHAPTER VIII

HOW LONG THE ALIENS WERE HELD IN PRISON

The Long Wait

By far the greater number of the men interviewed in Detroit had been in jail since the raids, which occured early in January. In fact, sixty-four of the eighty-two men seen by the investigator, on April 9 and 10, had been in custody over three months. Four men had been held since December, approximately four months, and two since early in November, over five months. One had been held for two months. In eleven cases the period of detention was not stated.

It is difficult to determine with precision the length of time that the various aliens whose records have been examined for the purpose of this record were held. This is because, first, some of the aliens were released on bail soon after their arrest, pending their hearings; second, others had warrants cancelled; third, still others after they had their hearings, if ordered deported, were released on bail pending deportation. In none of these three cases, however, was the date of release given and the immigration authorities had not received information as to the date when the alien was set free. In course of the regular procedure he may go out on bail pending the period of deportation, but in all of these cases no information is given as to the exact date on which the alien was released from custody. In fact cancellation of warrant was sometimes not followed by release until long after it had been promulgated.

Length of Detention Period

The following cases are illustrations of long detention periods:

Ignatz Maritzka (Warrant No. 54860/734) was arrested on January 3, 1920. The warrant for his arrest was issued on January 16th. Bond to the amount of $1,000 was asked which the alien was unable to furnish. Absence of evidence led to the cancellation of the warrant of this alien on April 1, 1920. He was therefore detained for a period of eighty-eight days.

Sam Kot (Warrant No. 54860/787) was arrested on or about January 15, 1920. His warrant was issued on January 17. The testimony and evidence presented at the hearing were such that the warrant was ordered cancelled on April 14. Since bail was set at one thousand dollars ($1,000) and the alien was unable to furnish it, he was held from the time of his arrest until after April 14. He was therefore detained for a period of ninety days.

Ivan Dudinsky (Warrant No. 54810/346) was arrested on or about January 3, 1920. His warrant was issued on December 29, 1919. Bond to the amount of ten thousand dollars ($10,000) was asked, which the alien was unable to furnish. Efforts were made to have the bail reduced, but without success. The case was closed on March 12, and ordered reopened on March 22. On April 12 bail was reduced to one thousand dollars, which was furnished and the alien was released on or about that date. He was therefore detained for a period of one hundred and one days. The alien had tuberculosis at the time.

Wasil Lalajo (Warrant No. 54709/190) was arrested on November 7, 1919, on warrant dated November 6. Bond was required to the amount of one thousand dollars which he was unable to furnish. A hearing was held on November 9, and the inspector made the following summary of findings:

> "Two of the special agents who have investigated Lalajo's case strongly recommend that the warrant be cancelled. In fact, they wanted me to release this alien last night, but owing to the fact that the warrant calls for a bond I did not feel like doing it without authority from the Department. I recommend that the work in this case be cancelled and that the Department notify the Inspector-in-Charge at Cleveland by telegraph that this alien can return to work and to support his family."

This statement was dated November 9, 1919. When the alien was visited in the Youngstown jail on April 8, 1920, five months, less one day, from the date of this recommendation Lalajo was still being detained. All warrant proceedings against this alien were cancelled eleven days later and if he was released immediately upon the cancellation of proceedings, he had been detained for a period of one hundred sixty-two days. His wife and children were meanwhile reported to be destitute and suffering.

The Question of Bail

After the hearing the aliens were disposed of in one of the following ways: If found "guilty" the alien was ordered deported; if found "not guilty" his warrant was cancelled; if his case was doubtful there were three possible courses: (1) proceedings were stayed from three to six months; (2) the alien released on parole with instructions to report to Government officials at certain intervals, (3) the case was ordered opened for a new hearing.

In case the alien was found "guilty" or proceedings were stayed, he might be released on bail pending deportation or a second hearing. Of the 200 aliens whose cases are reported in this account 95 actually furnished bail, and 35 were unable to furnish the amounts required. In the case of 17 the men were released on their own recognizance. In 52 cases it is not stated whether or not the amount was furnished and in one case the alien was paroled for one year.

It may be noted that there seems to have been no stated time at which the alien or his friends received official notice that he could be released on bail. In no case do we find a mention of the fact that the alien was given notice, according to rule, that he could be released on bail at the time of his preliminary examination.

The amount of bail required was recorded in one hundred eighty-one cases and ranged from $500 to $10,000. In 140 of these the amount of bail first required was $1,000, in the remaining 41 cases the amount originally required ranged from $1,500 to $10,000.

Instability of Bail

The reason is not always clear why bail was raised or reduced in given instances. There does appear to have been a great fluctuation in both amounts and subsequent raising or lowering of bail. In 18 cases the bail was raised from $1,000 all the way to $10,000. In one case, however, the amount was reduced from $1,000 to $500 and in two from $10,000 to $1,000. Two aliens who had originally been required to furnish $10,000 bail were released on their own recognizance, having been found not guilty of any offense.

Irregularity in Granting Bail

There are on record the names of twelve men who on April 7 had been out on bail for a month, some of them two months, and who on that date had not yet received receipt for the money furnished for bail. In one city the rumor was spread about that the receipt and the money would never be returned to the person furnishing the bond. This naturally resulted in making it impossible for others in custody to secure bail. In cases where the arrested men were unable to furnish bail, as well as in cases where bonds could be secured, many delays were incurred before final action was taken. In the case of George Luchin (Warrant No. 54860/189) the examination at Ellis Island was closed as early as January 24, but the record was not forwarded to Washington until March 3, more than five weeks later, the alien being all the time in custody under a bail exaction with which he was financially unable to comply. The warrant was cancelled in this case as soon as the data reached the authorities.

High Bail and the Aliens' Families

In 35 cases the aliens were unable to furnish bail. Ivan Efimenko (Warrant No. 54861/299) furnishes a typical example. This alien was a native of Russia, twenty-nine years of age and had been in this country for six years, was married and had three children, all born in this country. He resided at Flint, Michigan. He was arrested early in January and held until April 3, unable to furnish bond. He had been employed a few months prior to his arrest as a laborer with a motor car company and before that he had worked on a sugar beet farm near Flint, Michigan. Due to illness in the family and to other expenses he had been able to save only about $100 for the season's work. This amount was soon depleted and the family had no money or any one who could furnish it support. They were paying $18 a month for rent which they had been unable to meet for two months. A few neighbors and friends had made loans and gifts. They still owed $50.00 or more to the grocer. The family could not furnish the $5,000 bond required in this case. He was therefore kept in prison and the family was left without resources. The prisoner petitioned through his counsel to be released in order that he might provide for his family, promising to appear for hearings or deportation at any time that he was required to do so by the authorities.

On March 26, 1920, after the alien had been held for approximately three months, a Government representative sent the following wire to his department in Washington:

"Referring to case of Ivan Efimenko, Bureau File 54616/1. Please call for file and would advise wiring Doctor ———— authority to parole as he has requested several times. Matter serious."

The sufferings of the families of arrested aliens will be treated more fully in the following chapter.

CHAPTER IX

HOW THE ALIENS' FAMILIES WERE AFFECTED

Families of those Deported on the "Buford"

This report would not be complete without a statement concerning the families of those aliens who were deported on the "Buford," on December 21, 1919. We have learned that of thirteen women whose husbands were deported at that time, ten had children. Two of the thirteen women were pregnant.

In addition to the mental suffering, the economic distress caused by the sudden removal of the sole breadwinner of the family may readily be imagined. A few of these women had worked before their marriage, but the problem of immediately securing jobs was difficult because some provision had to be made for the children —some of them very young—during working hours. Offers of charity were consistently refused by these women, who uniformly asked for one thing—the privilege of joining their husbands, wherever they were.

In the case of Mrs. Michailoff, who was interviewed in connection with this investigation, the following facts were brought to light:

Mrs. Michailoff was a native of Russia, thirty years old. She had been in this country about eight years and had one child seven weeks old. She had never been employed prior to nor since her marriage. Her husband, who was a machinist, was arrested in Bayonne, N. J., in March, 1919. Mrs. Michailoff had visited her husband several times at Ellis Island, the last time about ten days before the "Buford" sailed. On that occasion he had asked for some clothes which she was able to secure through the American Workers Defense Union. When she went with them to Ellis Island she found the "Buford" had sailed. Mrs. Michailoff stated that the day before she had received a letter from her husband saying that he was going, he did not know where, and that he wanted to see her and their child again. At the time of a second interview with Mrs. Michailoff, she stated that she had found employment in one of Childs' restaurants as a dishwasher, for which she was receiving $9.00 per week. She said that she could not get along on this and was very desirous of joining her husband as soon as possible. She was staying with some friends and had not been able to pay them rent for two months.

In addition to these economic burdens, Mrs. Michailoff and her family had to bear the stigma of her husband's deportation as a radical. She said that her little boy came home from school one day crying and protesting that he would never go back, because the children ran after him and called him "Bolshevik."

Another woman who was left dependent by the deportation of her husband on the "Buford" was Mrs. Vincent Martzin. Mrs. Martzin is 22 years old, had a child of sixteen months and expected another within about a month from the time she was interviewed in March, 1920. She was left without money by her husband, who had only been able to secure irregular employment and since his deportation she had been dependent upon her sister who had two children and whose husband earned only $25 per week. Prior to the deportation of Mr. Martzin he stated that if he was found to be guilty under the law and deported he wanted his family to go with him. Mrs. Martzin learned that her husband was in Moscow and would have liked to join him there.

A third case was that of Mrs. Elsie Schatz, a native of Russia, 26 years old, and except for a period in 1914, when she returned to Russia to get her parents, has resided in this country since 1909. She was married in 1918. In March, 1919, her husband was arrested. At this time Mrs. Schatz was in a hospital. Her baby was born on March 4, but died on March 15. Her husband was released the day after his arrest, but was rearrested in July and again released the following day. He was arrested for the third time in November. A week from the date of his arrest his wife visited him for the first time at Ellis Island. In all she saw him four times. At the time of her husband's arrest in November, Mrs. Schatz was two months pregnant. After his arrest a miscarriage followed. Since that time Mrs. Schatz's health has not been good. She tried to find work to do but has had great difficulty in getting employment on account of her husband's deportation. Mrs. Schatz said during the interview that she would rather stay in this country, but wants to be with her husband, wherever he is.

Families of Those Held in Custody

In addition to the instances just cited where the women were permitted to see their husbands occasionally, the investigation disclosed that frequently prisoners were not allowed to see visitors and in many instances there came to our notice wives who were not allowed to see their husbands at all. One man, Fred Androchuk (Warrant No. 54809/297), who had not seen any member of his family since his arrest, was asked, "Who is taking care of your wife and children now?" "I don't know, they may be dead," he replied.

Prokpey Mojeika (Warrant No. 54860/3), one of the Detroit prisoners interviewed, seemed beside himself with anxiety over his wife and child. He did not belong to either of the proscribed organizations and professed to know no reason for his arrest. He said bitterly, "Wife goes from one house to another—no help." He said that if he were deported without his wife she would commit suicide. He asked to be set free or to be shot.

In Youngstown a charitable organization cared for the families of arrested men, but there seems to have been no uniform arrangement regarding this matter. Attached to one record was a letter from the United Charities of Chicago, stating that they had made an investigation of the family of one alien, Lookis Kozaced (Warrant No. 54859/472), and rendered necessary aid. Incidentally they discovered certain facts which, they said, led them to believe this prisoner should not be deported. The alien in question was a Pole, of excellent reputation, industrious and thrifty. He had taken out his first papers and bought two Liberty Bonds. The Superintendent of the United Charities of Chicago states that this alien had never been connected with any radical group. On January 2, at the invitation of Mr. Belensko (also investigated by the same organization) he had attended a meeting and was arrested while there. He was eventually released, his family having been cared for in the meantime. In other states, however, the aliens had no such assurance that the needs of their dependents were being provided for.

CHAPTER X

SUMMARY

In the foregoing papers are set forth the results of an inquiry into the deportations of 1919-1920 as represented in a cross section study, based on two hundred cases, together with the results of prison investigations. The facts have been presented in an objective manner, and the reader is left to draw his own deductions.

Personal History

We have found that these aliens were the common run of work-folk: store-keepers, shop-workers, shoe-makers, carpenters, mechanics, unskilled laborers and the like. Nearly two-thirds of them were Russians. Almost nine-tenths were between the ages of 20 and 40. They had resided in this country for a comparatively long period. Over half of them had families, most of whom were living in the United States and included American-born children. The large majority had a little knowledge of English, and many of them had made application for American citizenship papers. A few had served in the United States military forces, and most of them had purchased bonds or in other ways taken part in war-time activities.

Arrests

We find that they were arrested mostly in groups while attending meetings in public halls. In not a few cases there were no warrants of arrest until long after the apprehension. At the police stations or other places of detention, a number of the aliens appear to have been forced to sign statements which were later introduced as evidence against them. It is also clear that at first they were not permitted to see their relatives or friends. Some evidently received cruel and abusive treatment at the time of arrest and during the period of detention.

Hearings

A "trial" was in some cases not given them until weeks after they were imprisoned. Even at best their "trial" was, as provided by law, only an administrative hearing. In this proceeding the Immigrant Inspector, who was usually a man untrained in law and often without even an academic training, acted as prosecutor, judge and jury at the same time. Interpreters were often necessary because the aliens' knowledge of English was so imperfect. In some instances the very man who originally had caused the arrest of the alien acted as interpreter at the hearing. Frequently the accused was not informed of his right to counsel, and when he was so informed, it was done after the representatives of the government had extracted from him, sometimes by inquisitorial methods, all the admissions they desired.

Alleged Radicalism

This cross-section study reveals that only a small number of these aliens could be classed as dangerous radicals. A large number of them were transferred from the Socialist Party either without their knowledge or without understanding the significance of such a transfer. We find evidence that aliens were induced to join proscribed organizations through the efforts of a provocative agent. The simplicity of their testimonies, their obvious sincerity, their straightforwardness, testify to the fact that the majority of the persons involved in this study were simple-minded folk who entertained no purpose hostile to the American Government or the American people. When questioned with reference to their desire to remain in this country most of them expressed a preference not to be deported and said they would gladly abide by the laws of the United States.

Disposition of the 200 Cases

As indicated in the body of the report, of the 200 cases examined 175 final decisions had been rendered at the time this study was completed. Of these 97 called for cancellation of the warrant and 78 for deportation of the alien.

In this connection the statistics of deportation for the year July 1, 1919, to June 30, 1920, are interesting. During this period 2,777 aliens were deported for all causes, 314 of whom, or 11.3 per cent of the total, were of the classes considered in this report.

The Questions at Issue

It is a matter of common knowledge that the proportion of cancellations to the total number of warrants is very much greater than in the 200 cases here treated. The ground on which warrants were cancelled was usually a lack of evidence, in the judgment of the Assistant Secretary of Labor, who has been in charge of these cases, to prove either membership in a proscribed organization or a belief in violent opposition to government. The Assistant Secretary took the ground that only those who were members of the organization in question by free choice and who were informed as to the tenets of the organization, were deportable under the law and under the Secretary's ruling.

Recent Court Decisions

Two federal court decisions of contrary purport have been rendered in *habeas corpus* proceedings growing out of deportation cases, one by Judge Anderson of the U. S.

Circuit Court of Appeals, Boston, and the other by Judge Knox of the Southern District of New York. Judge Anderson has held that the Secretary of Labor erred in declaring membership in the Communist Party a sufficient ground for deportation, while Judge Knox's decision supports the Secretary's ruling. A decision on the cases in question is awaited from the Supreme Court.

Pending this decision it would scarcely be thought proper to refer more at length to these very interesting and important judicial opinions.

Hindrances to Deportation

Two reasons have been assigned for the fact that so few of those ordered deported have actually been sent abroad. First: Diplomatic relations between the United States and Russia were so abnormal as to make it exceedingly difficult, if not impossible, to deport the aliens, most of whom as we have seen were Russians, to Russia. Second: No transportation facilities were available directly into Russian territory and transportation by indirect routes was prohibitive in expense.

Social Consequences

Some of these aliens were held for a considerable period, which was virtually equivalent to an indeterminate sentence. A number were detained for weeks after they had been ordered released. In the meantime their families had been left without a means of support. As a consequence of all this a volume of prejudice and suspicion has been produced among immigrant groups, which it will require perhaps years to allay. It is impossible to know how much of the hostility now being reported on the part of foreign countries against America is due to the impressions made upon the nationals of other countries who have resided in the United States.

It is difficult to avoid the conclusion that, with the exception of the comparatively few persons who were clearly deportable under the law, these aliens needed not legal, but social and educational treatment, looking toward an effectual interpretation to them of the best ideals of American life.

APPENDIX I

EXCERPTS FROM THE DEPORTATION LAWS AFFECTING
ALIEN ANARCHISTS

Act of February 5, 1917

"SEC. 3. That the following classes of aliens shall be excluded from admission into the United States; . . . anarchists, or persons who believe in or advocate the overthrow by force or violence of the Government of the United States, or of all forms of law, or who disbelieve in or are opposed to organized government, or who advocate the assassination of public officials, or who are members of or affiliated with any organization entertaining and teaching disbelief in or opposition to organized government, or who advocate or teach the duty, necessity, or propriety of the unlawful assaulting or killing of any officer or officers, either of specific individuals or of officers generally, of the Government of the United States or of any other organized government, because of his or their official character, or who advocate or teach the unlawful destruction of property . . ."

"SEC. 19. That at any time within five years after entry, any alien who at the time of entry was a member of one or more of the classes excluded by law; any alien who shall have entered or who shall be found in the United States in violation of this act, or in violation of any other law of the United States; any alien who at any time after entry shall be found advocating or teaching the unlawful destruction of property, or advocating or teaching anarchy, or the overthrow by force or violence of the Government of the United States or of all forms of law or the assassination of public officials; . . . shall, upon the warrant of the Secretary of Labor, be taken into custody and deported . . ."

Act of October 16, 1918

"SEC. 1. That aliens who are anarchists; aliens who believe in or advocate the overthrow by force or violence of the Government of the United States or of all forms of law; aliens who disbelieve in or are opposed to all organized government;

aliens who advocate or teach the assassination of public officials; aliens who advocate or teach the unlawful destruction of property; aliens who are members of or affiliated with any organization that entertains a belief in, teaches, or advocates the overthrow by force or violence of the Government of the United States or of all forms of law, or that entertains or teaches disbelief in or opposition to all organized government, or that advocates the duty, necessity, or propriety of the unlawful assaulting or killing of any officer or officers, whether of specific individuals or of officers generally, of the Government of the United States or of any other organized government, because of his or their official character, or that advocates or teaches the unlawful destruction of property shall be excluded from admission into the United States."

"SEC. 2. That any alien, who at any time after entering the United States, is found to have been at the time of entry, or to have become thereafter, a member of any one of the classes of aliens enumerated in section one of this act, shall, upon the warrant of the Secretary of Labor, be taken into custody and deported. . . . The provisions of this section shall be applicable to the classes of aliens mentioned in this act, irrespective of the time of their entry. . . ."

"SEC. 3. Return to the United States after deportation is a felony and after punishment here, any alien so convicted shall again be deported."

APPENDIX II

A. *Nationality of the 200 Aliens*

Russians and Ukranians	148
Poles and Galicians	19
Lithuanians	9
Austrians	8
Croatians	6
Germans	3
Jugo-Slavs	2
Hungarians	2
Italian	1
Bulgarian	1
Dutch	1
Total	200

B. *Age of the 200 Aliens*

Under 20 years	2
20 to 25 "	46
26 to 30 "	62
31 to 35 "	48
36 to 40 "	23
41 to 45 "	9
46 to 50 "	4
Over 50 "	2
Age not given	4
Total	200

C. *Marital Status of the 200 Aliens*

Married	112
Single	83
Divorced	3
Not stated	2
Total	200

101

Aliens who had children 74
Aliens who had no children 29
Not stated 14

    TOTAL *117

Children born in U. S. 98
Children born abroad 37
Not stated 21

    Total number children involved 156

D. *Geographical Distribution of the 200 Aliens*

Connecticut 34
Georgia 1
Idaho 1
Illinois 33
Indiana 3
Maryland 4
Massachusetts 9
Michigan 31
Minnesota 3
Missouri 1
Nebraska 1
New Hampshire 9
New Jersey 19
New York 23
Ohio 7
Pennsylvania 10
Washington 6
Wisconsin 5

    TOTAL 200

---

* This total includes 112 married, 3 divorced, 2 not stated whether married or not.

TABLE I.—LENGTH OF RESIDENCE IN THE U. S. AND STATUS IN RELATION TO CITIZENSHIP

YEARS IN U.S.A.	TOTAL		STATUS IN RELATION TO CITIZENSHIP					
			APPLICATION FOR FIRST PAPERS MADE				NO APPLICATION MADE	NOT STATED
	NUMBER	PER CENT	TOTAL	GRANTED	REJECTED	NOT STATED		
Less than one year......	0							
1 year to five years......	31	15.5	8	4	3	1	14	9
6 years to 10 years......	134	67.0	30	17	6	7	91 (2)	13
11 years to 15 years......	23	11.5	13	11		2	9	1
16 years to 20 years......	7	3.5	2	1		1	3	2
21 years and over......	1	.5					1	
Not stated......	4	2.0	1		1 (1)		2	1
TOTAL......	200	100.0	54	33	10	11	120	26

(1) Application made but alien moved before granted.
(2) One of this group is a minor.

TABLE II.—ACTION TAKEN IN REFERENCE TO BAIL AND AMOUNT OF BAIL SET

ACTION	TOTAL	AMOUNT OF BAIL SET						
		1,000	1,500	2,000	2,500	5,000	10,000	Not Stated
Bail Furnished	94	81 (1)(2)	1	1 (3)	1	3 (5)	2	5
Unable to Furnish Bail	38	27			3 (4)	2 (5)	5 (6)	1
Released on own Recognizance	16	1					1	14
Released on Parole	1							1
Bail Set but Not Stated whether Furnished or not	41	18			1	1	21 (7)	
Nothing Recorded	10							10
TOTAL	200	127	1	1	5	6	29	31

(1) In one case in this group bail was set at $10,000 and later reduced to $1,000.

(2) In one case in this group bail was set at $1,000 and raised to $5,000 which the alien was unable to furnish, later reduced to $1,000.

(3) In one case in this group bail was set at $1,000 and raised to $2,000.

(4) In three cases in this group bail was set at $1,000 and raised to $2,500.

(5) In one case in this group bail was set at $1,000 and raised to $5,000.

(6) In three cases in this group bail was set at $1,000 and raised to $10,000.

(7) In five cases in this group bail was set at $1,000 and raised to $10,000.